T0023044

365 WAYS TO LIVE MINDFULLY

365 WAYS
TO LIVE MINDFULLY

BY PASCALE F. ENGELMAJER

First published in Great Britain by John Murray Learning in 2022
An imprint of John Murray Press
A division of Hodder & Stoughton Ltd,
An Hachette UK company

1

Copyright © Pascale Engelmajer 2022

The right of Pascale Engelmajer to be identified as the Author of the Work
has been asserted by her in accordance with the Copyright, Designs and
Patents Act 1988.

The acknowledgements on pp. 223 constitute an extension of this
copyright page.

A CIP catalogue record for this title is available from the British Library

Hardback ISBN 978 1 52939 039 1
eBook ISBN 978 1 52939 041 4

Typeset by KnowledgeWorks Global Ltd.

Printed and bound in Great Britain by Clays Ltd, Elcograf S.p.A.

John Murray Press policy is to use papers that are natural, renewable and
recyclable products and made from wood grown in sustainable forests.
The logging and manufacturing processes are expected to conform to the
environmental regulations of the country of origin.

John Murray Press
Carmelite House
50 Victoria Embankment
London EC4Y 0DZ

www.johnmurraypress.co.uk

To Max and Ziggy

CONTENTS

ABOUT THE AUTHOR

Pascale Engelmajer is Associate Professor of Religious Studies at Carroll University in Wisconsin. She is the author of *Women in Pāli Buddhism: Walking the Spiritual Path in Mutual Dependence* (Routledge), a book that examines women's spiritual agency, and *Buddhism* (Hodder & Stoughton), an introduction that provides an understanding of how doctrine informs practice in the contemporary Buddhist world. She has published widely on Buddhism for specialist and non-specialist audiences. She lives in Wisconsin with her family and engages in a daily practice that informs her writing.

INTRODUCTION

This book is about mindfulness, a state of consciousness in which your attention is focused on your present experience, without grasping, rejecting or judging it.

It is about helping you develop ways to live more mindfully, to be fully present to your life as it is right now, and to help you create a life that's consistent with your values and aspirations.

Being mindful is both very simple and very difficult.

It's simple because it requires nothing but your attention. Observe the thoughts, feelings and emotions in your mind. Observe the sensations in your body. Observe the world around you. Observe how you react to these experiences – do you want more of them? Less? Observe how you react to reacting to these experiences – do you feel happy? Annoyed? Angry? Ashamed? Observe that too.

That's being mindful. Pretty simple, isn't it? Now try it out. Pretty difficult, isn't it? This is what this book is about, walking the tightrope of mindfulness with grace and elegance.

But... what will you find in this book?

- Stories about people, such as the Buddha and his disciples, great masters in China, Tibet, Japan and other places, who lived in a more or less mythical past and have served as role models and sources of inspiration of mindful practice for countless people over time.

- Stories about people in the contemporary world, like the Dalai Lama or Thich Nhat Hanh, and others less well known who have made Buddhism and its insights, practices and wisdom accessible and relevant to modern life.

- Brief descriptions of Buddhist practices, concepts and principles whose goal is to foster mindfulness in all areas of life, from the meditation cushion (or chair) to brushing your teeth and washing the dishes.

■ Excerpts from the canonical texts of different Buddhist traditions: the Theravāda, the Southern Buddhist tradition practised in Sri Lanka, Thailand, Myanmar, Laos and Cambodia; the Mahāyāna, the Eastern tradition, practised in China, Korea, Japan and Vietnam; and the Vajrayāna, the Northern tradition of Tibet, Mongolia and Bhutan. And a few quotes from outside Buddhism too.

■ Brief descriptions of concepts and methods based on the latest research on mindfulness in modern psychology and neuroscience.

■ Many ideas, suggestions, tips, practices, exercises, prompts and habits to try out and cultivate.

■ Hopefully, a lot of inspiration, encouragement and support to help you on your journey to live in a more mindful way.

And... how can you use this book?

■ As a day-to-day source of inspiration and ideas about mindful living! As you see, the book has 365 entries organized into 13 chapters – 12 chapters that roughly correspond to each month of the year and one last chapter that includes the principles of mindfulness condensed to their fundamental essence. Each chapter is loosely based on a particular Buddhist virtue or principle, such as compassion, karma or patience. Start today: read the first entry and let it inspire you to live this day more mindfully. And then, tomorrow, read the second entry and so on and so forth. You have a full 365 days ahead!

■ Like a tarot deck! Instead of reading the entries chronologically, open the book at random and read an entry on that page. In this way, you have different virtues to explore every day – perhaps you can take the entry as your suggestion for the day?

■ Like fortune sticks! In many Asian countries, you can find fortune sticks in temples. Typically, you ask a question and shake the container holding the sticks until one falls out. The number on the stick tells you which 'page' to read for an answer to your question. You might try shaking the book but (hopefully) no page will fall out. Ask a question anyway, open the book at random, and let the page help you see your question in a different light and discover your own answers.

■ As a mindfulness boost! You can use every chapter, and the last one especially, when you need a general mindfulness boost. The last chapter contains five core ideas that distil the ideas and practical suggestions contained in the book into five fundamental points to nurture your mindful living.

Whichever way you choose to use this book (and you can sample them all!), try the exercises, suggestions and prompts you will find in it. Like any skill, mindfulness works only when you put it into practice. You would not learn how to fly a plane by only reading a book. Here, too, you want to put in the hours. Try one exercise, try a couple, try them all, but do try them.

As you find those that work well for you, add them to your toolbox and keep practising them until they become part of you.

There are many different practices in this book, and you're bound to find many that will resonate with you and will allow you to be a more mindful you. Although they are all ultimately related to each other, they can all be practised independently.

It is my wish that you will find something beneficial and effective in this book and that it will contribute to making your life more mindful, more present and more fulfilling.

CHAPTER 1
INTENTION

1   You're already there

The Buddha once said that he taught 'suffering and the end of suffering'. He called the journey from one to the other the Noble Eightfold Path.

It is a long journey. Tradition has it that it took over 500 lives for the Buddha to complete it.

It is also the shortest journey. The Buddha teaches that, if we could be mindful for just one instant, we would reach the end of suffering in that same instant. We have already arrived.

Each of the eight 'limbs' of the Buddhist path is simply an aspect of the same truth: we are already there. Understanding that we are already there is what takes time. And so, we must make the journey.

The eight limbs work together to take us to the end of suffering. Once we have the road map (Right View), we can set our destination (Right Intention) and start walking (Right Speech, Right Action, Right Livelihood, Right Effort), checking that we are on the correct path (Right Mindfulness) and going at the appropriate pace (Right Concentration).

For those of us who need a little more hand-holding (I know I do), the Buddha taught the 'step-by-step discourse', a condensed description of the Eightfold Path that focuses on developing morality, contemplation and wisdom.

Where are you at? The first step on *any* path is to recognize and fully accept where you are right now. Or, in other words, to be mindful of the present moment.

See? You've already arrived.

2   A road map

In Buddhist thinking, Right View is both the guide for all the other aspects of the Noble Eightfold Path and the culmination of the path, whereby you attain the full understanding of 'things as they are' that characterizes awakening (*nirvāṇa*).

Right View is like a road map: it tells you the direction you should take to arrive at your destination. It also implies that suffering comes from 'wrong views', all the preconceptions and prejudices of which you are often only barely aware but which drastically impact how you live your life. Imagine picking the wrong map to guide your journey!

In another sense, Right View represents our need for meaning.

3   Find the people who inspire you

According to the Buddhist texts, Sumedha was an ancient incarnation of the Buddha who vowed to become a fully awakened buddha for the benefit of all beings. The story tells us that Sumedha had been practising ascetism for many years when he heard that Buddha Dīpamkara (an earlier buddha) was visiting nearby.

When Sumedha saw Dīpamkara, he was struck by his countenance and the immense compassion that emanated from him. Sumedha thought, 'Today, I could attain awakening and end my own suffering, but I have the extraordinary chance to meet a buddha. What if I made the vow of also becoming a buddha to inspire and help others to bring about the end of their own suffering?' He threw himself at the feet of Buddha Dīpamkara and vowed to practise the qualities of the spiritual path until he reached full awakening as a buddha.

Who has inspired you to grow and become your better self, just as Buddha Dīpamkara's great compassion inspired Sumedha to become the Buddha of our times?

4   Find your intention

What is your intention? What would you like to achieve? What do you want your life to mean? What goals would you like to realize? You can think about today, tomorrow, next month, next year or your whole life.

As an exercise now, write about your intention in the different areas of your life (personal, health, emotional, social and professional). Take your journal, or a piece of paper if you prefer, and explore your life intentions. Be as specific and descriptive as you can and as imaginative as you wish.

Don't hesitate to make bold statements.

5   A Resolution

My body, every possession
And all goodness, past, present and future
Without remorse I dedicate
To the wellbeing of the world.

Śāntideva (685–763 CE), *The Bodhicaryāvatāra*

6   Cultivate Right Intention

Buddhist texts say that Right Intention has three main aspects: the intention of renunciation, the intention of benevolence and the intention of not harming.

Renunciation can be understood as giving up unhealthy attachments and desires, the kinds that lead to discontent and sorrow – think toxic relationships, unhealthy foods or unbridled consumerism.

Benevolence, or goodwill, can be understood as the intention to actively develop kind and compassionate ways of being in the world. This, in turn, is related to the intention of not harming – including not harming yourself, other people, non-human animals and the environment.

What does your own Right Intention look like?

7   Meet the Buddha

The historical figure of the Buddha is said to have been born a prince named Siddhartha around 2,500 years ago in the north-east of the Indian subcontinent, in a town called Kapilavastu (now in southern Nepal).

Although he had a life of wealth and privilege, Siddhartha grew dissatisfied. The tradition represents this dissatisfaction with the Four Sights that Siddhartha encountered on visits outside the palace precinct: a sick man, an old man, a corpse and a renouncer. These sights motivated him to seek an end to the suffering intrinsic to existence that they symbolized.

He abandoned the lavish lifestyle of his royal palace to pursue a path of renunciation that led him to experience awakening (*nirvāṇa*), a profound transformation of his understanding of the nature of existence and his relationship to it. He became a buddha, an awakened being, and a teacher who established the *Sangha*, a community of monks, nuns, and lay men and women.

Whether or not you believe in the story of the Buddha, what do you make of its symbolism and significance? What transformative experiences impacted how you live your life?

8   Live your values

Living your values imbues your life with meaning. Too often we get caught up in the routine and busyness of everyday life and lose sight of what really matters to us. To live your values, or to put it another way, to 'practise what you preach', examine your behaviour in light of your values.

Whether you do this on a daily, weekly or monthly basis, make a habit of reminding yourself of what your most important values are. Pinpoint clearly how your daily actions express those values. You can schedule a daily, weekly or monthly slot of time to dedicate to this reflection.

After you have practised this for a while, it will become second nature. You will find yourself being more intentional about what actions to take or avoid, and more confident that your actions embody your values.

9   The glow of awakening

After the Buddha reached *nirvāṇa*, he wanted to share his realization with the six companions with whom he had spent many years performing ascetic practices and discussing philosophical issues.

While he was searching for them, he met a man who, surprised at the Buddha's glowing and almost supernatural appearance, asked him, 'Who are you? What are you? A spirit or a god?'

The Buddha replied that he was a buddha, one who has attained awakening and transcended the suffering of ordinary existence. The man, not particularly impressed, scoffed at the Buddha's revelation and went on his way.

Sometimes we meet the teacher we need but we are not quite ready to hear their insight. Have you had the experience of not resonating with something or someone upon first meeting them and then later being transformed by the encounter? How did it feel?

10   Set a daily intention

When you wake up, or at a convenient time in the morning, maybe with your morning tea or coffee or while you are in the shower, think about your day and set an intention for yourself.

It can be a practical intention such as 'I intend to exercise for at least 30 minutes today' or 'I'll clear my email inbox this morning'. Or it can be a mental habit such as 'I intend to be more attentive today by noticing the environment around me on my way to work, or by being considerate to the cashier at the coffee shop, looking at them in the eyes and smiling' or 'I intend to be more self-compassionate and acknowledge that, like all human beings, I am not perfect'.

Remind yourself to check throughout the day how you're keeping up with this daily intention. No need to judge; just observe what happens.

11   The sick man, the old man, the corpse and the renouncer

In South-East Asia, visual representations of the Buddha's life are found everywhere, from murals on temple walls to comic books in supermarket aisles. A favourite is the depiction of the Four Sights which Siddhartha (the future Buddha) encountered when he went out of the royal palace precinct with his charioteer, Channa.

According to the texts, the young prince had led a privileged life, shielded from suffering, and this was the first time that he saw sickness, old age and death. Understanding that these are unavoidable caused him to have an existential crisis only barely softened by the fourth sight, the serene and tranquil renouncer. Shaken by his realization, Siddhartha abandoned the palace, his young wife and infant son to pursue the spiritual path that culminated in his awakening.

Whether or not you believe in its historical accuracy, the story illustrates, in a vivid and dramatic way, the inevitable reality of existence and how you can be inspired to reconsider your values and life choices when, like Siddhartha, you realize the limited and impermanent nature of existence.

12   What are your values?

Buddhism's foundational values are compassion and wisdom. The entirety of Buddhist principles, sacred texts and practices stems from these two overarching values. They are said to imbue the Buddha's every action.

Take a moment to reflect on your values and, when you are ready, make a list of what they are. Why are they important to you? How do you put them into practice? How could you put them into practice more intentionally in your daily life?

Be specific and detailed in your description. Don't hesitate to give examples and to draw on memories or role models.

13   A story of intentions: Māyā, the Buddha's mother

The story of Māyā, the Buddha's mother, gives an insight into the power of intentions. Māyā is the perfect mother who gave her life for the baby Buddha. She carried him in her womb, and after he was born, she died and was reborn in a heavenly realm where she reached awakening. This is the story told most frequently in Buddhist lore.

But there is another way to understand Māyā's story, especially when we look at the stories of her previous lives. There Māyā shows her true colours: the stories tell us that a very long time ago, in a previous life, she vowed to become the mother of a future buddha. Through each of her successive lives, she endeavoured to cultivate the qualities that led her to be reborn as Māyā. She prepared herself morally and spiritually for bearing the future Buddha, engaging in ascetic and spiritual practices, and offering a role model through her generosity and ethical behaviour.

Taken in its totality, with its many stories, the legend of Māyā shows us how intentions, over time, guide us to our goals. When, like Māyā, have you worked towards a long-term goal? How did you keep in mind your initial intention?

14   Implement your values

Your intentions are motivated by your values whether you are aware of it or not. Of course, they are also affected by the circumstances in which you find yourself.

While you cannot always do much to change your circumstances, you can reflect on your values and identify those important to you. In that way, you can ensure that your actions are consistent with the values that matter most to you.

A good practice is to identify a set of three foremost values and reflect on how you implement them in your life. Are your daily actions consistent with these values? If not, how can you act differently so that you become more attuned with them?

15   Is this the person you want to be?

Before doing or saying anything, especially if your actions or words have an impact on another person, make a habit of asking yourself: Does this action reflect who I am? Does it put my values into practice? Does it represent what I stand for?

Another way of examining your actions is to ask: Is this the person I want to be?

If you can answer yes to these questions, go ahead. If not, reconsider and find a behaviour or words that better match your values.

16   You are human

Much personal development focuses on efforts to change. But for any change to happen, you must have a clear view of who you already are.

Think about it: if you're trying to go to Paris, you need to know where you're starting from.

So, where are you starting from? Who are you? Be honest with yourself, but be gentle too. Typically, we want to change because we are not content with who we are. Your task is to practise adopting a dispassionate view and seeing yourself exactly as you are – a human being with qualities and flaws, like any other human being.

Embrace who you are. Celebrate your qualities. Accept your shortcomings. Yes! Accept your shortcomings, even those you most dislike about yourself. Embrace them. They make you human.

Breathe deeply and rest in the feeling that you are okay as you are. Really.

17   Go public

Every other week, Buddhist monks and nuns recite the rules of monastic life. They publicly announce their intention to follow these rules and they hold each other accountable for upholding them.

Research shows that when you make your intentions public, you are much more likely to achieve your goals. A challenge is to share your goals with a friend, or a group of friends, who will be both supportive and demanding. They will encourage you and prod you to live up to your intentions, and they will support you when you don't because they know that we all fail sometimes.

18   Be who you want to be

In the 1990s, psychologist Steven Hayes developed acceptance and commitment therapy (ACT). Although it is not based on Buddhist principles, ACT's understanding of certain psychological processes resembles that found in Buddhist psychology.

One main concept is that psychological health depends on accepting things as they are. For ACT, the basis for change is recognizing our life and circumstances as they are and accepting even those things we most wish to change as a starting point. In Buddhist psychology, the basis for change is recognizing that suffering is unavoidable not because you, or the world, are inherently bad, but because of the way you relate to yourself and to the world.

Once you accept this, you can start progressing on the path. This shared insight highlights that accepting yourself *as you are*, fully and unconditionally, is the first step towards being who you want to be.

And seriously… you don't have a choice.

19   Like one's own shadow

We are the result of our thoughts and are driven by our thoughts.

Sorrow follows one who acts or speaks out of evil intentions, as the wheel follows the foot of the ox. …

Happiness follows one who acts or speaks out of good intentions, like one's own shadow.

The Buddha, *The Dhammapada*, verse 1

20   See yourself from the outside in

It is not easy to have an accurate sense of who you are as a person. We tend to see ourselves as better or worse than we actually are, especially because we are obviously privy to the content of our own mind – all the thoughts and emotions that are part of our mental weather, even though we may never act on them.

In this exercise, try to step outside of yourself and see what others might see, from a realistic and gentle perspective. What kind of person are you? What qualities do you have? What flaws? Be honest and kind. The goal is not to be self-critical (there is already enough of that in your mind). The goal is to paint a realistic picture and foster acceptance of yourself as the human being you are.

Finish the description with accepting words such as 'I am a typical human being. I have qualities and flaws'. Or any statement that you find comforting and supportive.

21   Buddha, buddha and buddhas

The term 'buddha' refers to any being who has attained awakening (*nirvāṇa*). In the same way that the term 'christ' (a title that means 'anointed' in ancient Greek) has become the main way of referring to Jesus, 'buddha' refers to Siddhartha Gautama, the man who reached awakening and taught the Buddhist path in the fifth century BCE.

Although European languages such as English or French use the term 'Buddha' (with a capital b to differentiate it from the simple title), the Buddhist texts use many terms to address or speak about the Buddha, such as teacher (*Satthar*) and blessed one (*Bhagavat*). These terms express the great reverence and veneration in which those who composed the Buddhist texts held the Buddha as the being who not only discovered the path to awakening but also taught it to others.

In later Buddhism, especially Mahāyāna Buddhism, the idea developed that the historical Buddha was one buddha among an infinite number of buddhas. All buddhas reside in their own buddha realm and are accessible at all times to provide help and support to all beings, as the historical Buddha did when he established Buddhism in our world.

22   Like every other human being

Psychologist Kristin Neff, who researches the concept of self-compassion based on Buddhist principles, recommends that we treat ourselves as we would a best friend. In difficult times, especially those times when we would usually berate ourselves harshly, she advises us to remember that we are fallible human beings, like every other human being.

Accepting that we are not perfect, that we have flaws and that we make mistakes, her research has uncovered, helps us deal better with difficult situations and energizes us.

When the voice of self-criticism grates in your ear, remind yourself that making mistakes and being imperfect is just human. Show yourself kindness and understanding as you would a dear friend.

23   Radical intentions: Venerable Chao Hwei's bodhisattva path

Venerable Chao Hwei's work demonstrates that the practice of Buddhism extends beyond the doors of the monastery to all aspects of social life, including human interaction with the non-human world. In February 2021, she was awarded the 38th Niwano Peace Prize in recognition of 'her work in peace-building through her safeguarding of all forms of life, her promotion of gender ethics, gender equality, and her approach to open-minded dialogue with different religious leaders and social groups'.

Chao Hwei, who was born in Burma in 1957, has lived in Taiwan since she was ten. She chose the monastic life after finishing university, becoming what she calls a 'social campaigner for human rights, gender equality, environmental conservation and animal protection'. She provided support for prisoners on death row, performed the first same-sex wedding ceremony in Taiwan and demonstrated publicly for equal rights for Buddhist nuns. She is also an ardent animal rights activist, arguing that human beings have a moral duty to treat other animals in more humane ways.

In very practical ways, Venerable Chao Hwei fulfils her bodhisattva vow (her vow to become a fully awakened buddha for the benefit of all beings) as she works tirelessly to transform society by challenging systemic inequalities.

How do you fulfil your intentions?

24   WOOP for joy

Psychologist Gabriele Oettingen and her colleagues developed a step-by-step approach to setting and achieving one's life goals, big and small. They called it WOOP, for Wish, Outcome, Obstacle and Plan. Oettingen's research showed that when people engaged in WOOP on a consistent basis, they identified authentic and realistic goals that they were then able to realize.

The four steps require you to identify truly authentic goals (Wish) by imagining what it would feel like to have achieved them (Outcome), recognizing the internal obstacles that may come up (Obstacle) and outlining ways of dealing with these obstacles (Plan). The steps must be followed in this exact order to be successful, and the process demands that you be genuine and clear about your wishes and internal obstacles.

Oettingen recognizes that, at first, it takes time to put the sequence into practice, but she says that after a while it becomes a habit that can help you identify goals that are truly yours and achieve them.

Now go WOOP!

25   The seed of awakening

In the *Tathāgatagarbha Sūtra*, a third-century CE Mahāyāna sutra (a text considered to have been composed or inspired by an awakened being, typically the Buddha himself), the Buddha declares that we all have buddha-nature. Regardless of how bad we may think we are, there is a seed within us that contains the possibility of awakening.

The concept of buddha-nature is very important in Eastern Buddhism. In essence, it reminds us that we all share an inherent goodness and that, because all beings possess this inherent goodness, we should treat them with kindness and compassion.

In fact, this inherent goodness is your buddha-nature, your true nature. How do you seek to actualize it?

26 Identify your goals

Psychological research shows that people who identify goals that are personal, concrete, specific and positive are more likely to achieve them. Identify one or two goals in one area of your life that you want to achieve. Make sure they are personal (they are truly yours, not imposed on you), concrete and specific (you can clearly see when you have achieved them), and positive (they are based on action, not on *not doing*).

For example, such a goal could be: 'This year, I will be more active. I will… [walk, jog, run, exercise, do yoga, skip, dance…] at least 30 minutes every day. In addition, whenever possible, I will walk or cycle instead of driving. I will schedule several walking breaks during the day, such as having walking meetings and using the stairs instead of the elevator.'

Take time to describe clearly how you will implement your goals in positive and specific details. Of course, you can do this with every area of your life – don't stop at health and fitness.

27 A precious human life

A very popular poem attributed to Tenzin Gyatso, the 14th Dalai Lama, exhorts us to reflect, as we wake up, about how fortunate we are to be alive.

We should consider that being alive is a privilege that we should not waste. We should use our energy to develop ourselves and to expand our hearts to others, by having kind thoughts and not getting angry.

A human life is precious, and we should use it to benefit others as much as we can.

How do you make your life count?

28   A gold star

The goal here is to be mindful about the good things that you do: write down the good habits, practices, attitudes and behaviours that you usually don't pay attention to and recognize them explicitly. This is your buddha-nature shining through.

Take a moment to think back on the past week and focus on the good you've done. What are you proud of? Have you achieved the goals you had set for yourself? Have you finished a task that had been on your plate for too long? Have you kept a promise? Have you been generous or cheerful even when it was not easy? Have you done what you had to do even when you didn't feel like it? What intentions did you have that you were able to follow through?

Now, give yourself a pat on the back, a gold star, a piece of chocolate or whatever you wish to celebrate the good you did this week.

29   Keep your word

Who has never made a promise that they then were reluctant to keep? I wish I could say I had!

You can develop a habit of asking yourself before you make a promise or take on a commitment, 'Will I still want to do this at the time I'm supposed to do it? Will I have the time? Will I have the resources?'

If you can emphatically reply positively to these questions, go ahead and make a promise. If not, consider alternatives which you would be more comfortable with. It may be easier for you to accept now, but it is better to refuse or to offer another option than to put yourself in a position to be unreliable.

30　Realize a goal from beginning to end

This is your challenge. Pick a short-term goal (especially one that has been on your to-do list for a long time). Using WOOP, the strategy developed by Gabriele Oettingen, make a plan to realize your goal.

Remember to clearly describe your Wish, its Outcome, the internal Obstacles (those that are dependent on you, not on other factors) and the Plan to address the obstacles and achieve your goal.

It is possible that you will realize that this goal is not an authentic and personal goal, or that the obstacles that prevent you from realizing it are not in your control. This is good. It won't weigh on you anymore!

You can cross it off your list and move on to the next one.

CHAPTER 2

WISDOM

31   Get on with it

When the Buddha said that 'existence is suffering', he was telling us to look life squarely in the eyes. We live as though now is not our 'real' life but a preparation for it, as though, at some point, life will be perfect: no more headaches, no more worries, no more heartbreaks, no more arguments, no more failures.

In the first Noble Truth of suffering, the Buddha states that we can't avoid physical and mental pain regardless of what we hope for or do. Neither can we avoid the suffering caused by impermanence and change, by the fact that nothing lasts for ever and that everything, including ourselves, changes.

Impermanence at its core is the truth that life is finite. We *will* die. Not only will we die but our options are limited by our historical, sociocultural, economic and biological circumstances. And to top it all, there is very little we can control.

The Buddha was telling us: 'That's it! This is the life you're living! Get on with it!'

32   The truth of suffering

This is the noble truth of suffering. Birth is suffering. Ageing is suffering. Sickness is suffering. Death is suffering. Sorrow, grief, pain, unhappiness and discomfort is suffering. The presence of what we don't like is suffering. The absence of what we like is suffering. Not getting what we want is suffering. In brief, existence is suffering.

The Buddha, *Samyutta Nikāya*, V 421

33   What causes you suffering?

The middle of the night is the time when worries and fears visit me. I wake up around two or three in the morning and I think about all the things that went wrong or those that might, the missed opportunities, the blunders, the too much work, the not enough time off, our children's future, the pandemic, the state of the economy, the state of the world. The list is infinite.

I have learned that my mind will *always* find something to worry about, and it is usually something I can do absolutely nothing about.

I find the following exercise useful. Take a pen and write about the things that wake you up at night or that stop you from truly enjoying life. As you list them, ask yourself what about each thing you wish to be different. Further ask yourself what you can do to control it.

If you can do something, write that down too. If you cannot do anything, release the thought.

34   Like a mirror

One day, when Rahula, the Buddha's son, had just become a monk, the Buddha visited him and gave him advice on how to conduct himself.

'Rahula,' he asked, 'what is the purpose of a mirror?'

'For the purpose of reflection, venerable sir,' replied Rahula.

'Rahula, be like a mirror,' the Buddha pursued, 'before you take action, reflect in this way: "Is this action for my benefit and for that of others? Will the result of this action be positive or negative?" If your action is beneficial to you and others and its results positive, go ahead and do it. But, if the action is not beneficial and its results are negative, don't do it.'

Be like Rahula and, before you act, ask yourself, 'Are my actions beneficial to myself and others and will they have positive results?'

35   Why do we suffer?

'Why do we suffer?' you might want to ask sometimes. According to the Buddhist second Noble Truth, we experience suffering because of craving. Craving in turn leads to attachment. Think about it: we want health, wealth and happiness, but we don't always get these things. And when we do, we fear losing them or we don't enjoy them as much as we expected. This causes us anxiety and worry – what the Buddhists call suffering.

On the other hand, there are many things we don't want. We don't want to be living in a pandemic or in times of political and social divisiveness. We don't want our loved ones to get sick or die. We don't want to lose our job. And yet these things happen and cause us tremendous sorrow.

All things change and eventually end. The sun rises and sets. Flowers bloom and wilt. Emotions rise and dissolve. We, and those we love, will grow old and die.

When we crave things to be other than they are, we suffer. When we accept them the way they are, we live more mindfully.

36   Embrace boredom

How often have you reached for your phone when waiting at the doctor's office? At a red light? In the restroom? We can't even bear one or two minutes of boredom without trying to relieve it.

In experiments at Harvard University and at the University of Virginia, researchers found that test subjects would rather zap themselves with an electric current than remain without any distraction for even just a few minutes.

In the second Noble Truth, the Buddha explains that we crave objects of the senses. We want food, pleasant things to see, hear, touch and smell, but more than anything we crave objects of the mind. In other words, we want to be constantly entertained.

The digital technology industry has zoomed into our constant desire for entertainment and promises to satisfy every craving we have. The moment we feel bored or dissatisfied with our current experience, we turn to our devices (or to electric current!) to distract us. What they do really is distract us from living our life just as it is.

Embrace boredom! Develop the practice to be here and now. You may well discover the real world out there.

37 *Nirvāṇa*

Nirvāṇa is a term that has become part of contemporary languages outside of its original Buddhist context. Like *karma*, it is often misunderstood. *Nirvāṇa* is not some sort of dull and mindless happy-ever-after, or a drug-like daze. Instead, *nirvāṇa*, the third Noble Truth of Buddhism, refers to both a cognitive and affective attitude towards reality.

On the one hand, *nirvāṇa* is the full understanding of the nature of existence – life sometimes sucks, bad stuff happens, even to good people, and at the end of it we die anyway. Or, to put it in more Buddhist terms, existence is suffering because it is impermanent, always changing and ultimately unsatisfactory.

On the other hand, *nirvāṇa* is a profound change in the way we relate to reality: we both let it go *and* embrace it fully. We let go of expecting things to be different from what they are and we embrace them exactly as they are.

38 Nothing whatsoever

Nothing differentiates *saṃsāra* from *nirvāṇa*, nothing whatsoever
Nothing differentiates *nirvāṇa* from *saṃsāra*, nothing whatsoever
The limit of *nirvāṇa* is the limit of *saṃsāra*.
Between the two, there is not the slightest bit of difference.

Nāgārjuna (c. 150–250), *Madhyamakākarikā*, 25: 19–20

39   Let it go

Here is an exercise for the times when you feel overwhelmed by anxiety.

Breathe deeply into the anxiety, trying to feel it in your body – where do you feel it? In your throat? Chest? Stomach? Lower abdomen? How does it feel? Is it warm? Cool? Fuzzy? Solid? There is no judgement, just observation.

Then ask yourself: Do you have control over this thing that worries you? If you have control over it, what can you do about it? Thank the anxiety for bringing this to your attention, make a note of how and when to address the issue, and let it go.

If you don't have control over it, then you don't need to worry. Again, thank the anxiety for bringing this to your attention and resolve to let it go.

40   Nāgārjuna visits the *nāga* kingdom

When Nāgārjuna (*c.* 150–250 CE) was born, his parents received a prediction that the only way to prevent their son's early demise was to send him to a Buddhist monastery. The young Nāgārjuna loved learning and became so knowledgeable, the legend says, that the king of the *nāgas* (mythical sea serpents) invited him to work as a teacher at his court.

While in the *nāga* kingdom, Nāgārjuna discovered the *Perfection of Wisdom* sūtras, said to have been lost since the Buddha had taught them many centuries before. Nāgārjuna brought them back to the human realm and started the Buddhist Madhyamika school of philosophy, deeply influencing the development of Mahāyāna Buddhism, predominantly found today in East Asia.

Nāgārjuna's claim that there is no difference between *nirvāṇa* and *saṃsāra* prompted some of his contemporaries to accuse him of destroying Buddhism but, according to the philosopher, *nirvāṇa* is not an alternative reality separate from everyday life. Rather, once you realize the interdependent nature of all things, you realize *nirvāṇa* here and now.

41   Recognize impermanence

As an exercise, take your journal and jot down what arises when you reflect on the impermanence of those you love, of yourself, of the current circumstances (as I write we are entering our third year of the Covid-19 pandemic). There will be an end to good things, and there will be an end to bad things. How does the fact that everything changes make you feel?

Take your time and consider also how it changes your attitude towards those close to you, towards yourself, towards events like the pandemic. How does shifting your perspective impact you?

Describe what you can do differently to bring this shift of perspective into your daily life.

42   See the doctor

The Buddha compared himself to a physician. He diagnosed the disease. He identified its cause. He determined its cure and prescribed the treatment. The treatment for the disease of suffering is the Buddhist path (the Noble Eightfold Path), which essentially encompasses the entirety of life: our behaviour, our understanding of the world and our interaction with it.

Think of the aspects of the path as the areas that constitute your daily experience and as guideposts that help you reframe how you live. Right

View asks you to reflect on how you understand the world around you – are you seeing what is there? Or are you seeing what you hope or want to see?

Similarly, Right Intention encourages you to consider what motivates you in your daily life, your work and your relationships. Right Speech, Right Action and Right Livelihood help you focus on congruence between your values and your behaviour – are your words and activities consistent with your values? In other words, are you practising what you preach? Right Effort asks you if you are overexerting yourself or, on the contrary, not applying enough energy to what matters to you. Finally, Right Mindfulness and Right Concentration direct you inwards to evaluate if, and how, you are focusing on what matters in the present moment.

43   Are you sure?

We are often convinced that what we know is true. But we usually perceive only a part of reality. Like the proverbial blind men examining an elephant, we think the elephant is a tree because we have only touched her leg, or we think she is a snake because we have only felt her trunk.

In the same way, we think a person may have wronged us because we have only seen them swerve in front of us, not the emergency they're facing. Or we think that another one is a liar even though we have, in fact, heard only part of what they said.

Right View, the first aspect of the Eightfold Path, encourages us to develop the habit of questioning everything we think we know and to ask ourselves: Am I sure? Do I have all the information I need here? Can I take another perspective on this?

Every time you think you can pass a judgement, ask yourself these questions.

44   When you wash rice, wash rice: the teachings of Dōgen

One day, when he was young, the Japanese monk Eihei Dōgen (1200–1253) was on a ship to China when an elderly monk came aboard and bought some mushrooms. Dōgen enquired about the reason for the purchase and the monk explained that he was the *tenzo* (cook) at Mount Ayuwang monastery. The mushrooms were for the monks' evening meal.

Surprised, Dōgen wanted to know why such an elderly monk was spending time cooking instead of meditating or studying the sacred texts of the ancient masters. The monk laughed and replied that Dōgen did not understand yet the meaning of practice.

Dōgen became a Zen master who established the Japanese Sōtō Zen school. Although he was born into an aristocratic family in Kyoto's imperial court, the early loss of his parents led him to reject his inheritance of a high position at court and at 14 he ordained as a monk. Spurred by his inquisitive mind, he travelled to China where he met Rujing, a Caodong master, who taught a rigorous form of Zen, called *zazen*, 'just sitting' meditation. Dōgen brought this austere form of Buddhism to Japan, where it remains one of the dominant schools.

Dōgen was a prolific writer who, taking up the lesson from the elderly monk he had met on the ship, insisted that daily activities were part of the spiritual practice, advising 'when you wash rice and prepare vegetables, you must do so with your own hands, and with your own eyes, making sincere efforts'.

For Dōgen, we should pay as much attention to everyday activities as we do to meditation.

45   Heaven knows I'm miserable now!

You might have recognized the title of this song. If you don't know it, check it out. The song is a bitter illustration of the Buddhist second Noble Truth of suffering: the singer wants a job, gets it and then realizes, 'Heaven knows I'm miserable now!' He enjoys getting drunk but then pays for it with a hangover. He sees lovers and resents them for their happiness.

We too suffer from comparing our situation to that of others. We want what we don't have. We're not satisfied with what we *do* have. We engage in activities that have negative consequences. While Morrissey is more than a tad bleak in this song, we all, at some point or another, exclaim, 'I'm so miserable.'

Notice when you look at your life with miserable lenses and change them for more accurate ones.

46   Do you need a break?

Sometimes you feel you need a break. You want to take the day off, or maybe just an hour. But you have a deadline looming, or a pile of laundry. Or you need to get to work. Sometimes, you're really aching for that break and you do deserve it. How can you decide whether you're just being lazy or whether you've reached that breaking point (pun intended)?

Try this: Will you feel better if you take the break? Or will you feel worse? What kind of break will it be? Scrolling through social media on your phone? Or going for a walk? Which of these will help you feel restored and re-energized?

Be candid. Sometimes getting on with work (or laundry) makes you feel better about yourself. Sometimes a walk is what is needed. If you pay attention and are honest with yourself, you can find an answer that helps you live more mindfully.

47　Hell is other people

French writer and philosopher Jean-Paul Sartre wrote: 'Hell is other people.' He was both right and wrong. Think about it. Almost all your happiness and suffering depend on your relationships.

The idea of interdependence highlights how important others are to our wellbeing. Yet, we know we cannot control what others do or say. We do, however, control what *we* do or say.

When you feel dissatisfied or let down, think about what you would want your relationship to be like, then do what is required. For example, do you wish your friend would call or text you? Call or text them! Do you wish your partner would remember what your favourite food is? Always remember what *theirs* is.

Resolve to *be* the friend or partner *you* want to have.

48　Look at a flower

Take a flower. Look at it carefully. What do you see?

Zen teacher Thich Nhat Hanh tells us that all is contained in a simple flower. A flower contains the universe – the soil, the air, the sun and the water that made it grow and bloom. A flower does not exist independently of everything else. This is emptiness, *śūnyatā*.

The concept of emptiness is complex, and countless treatises have been written about it. At its core, the idea that all things are empty means that all things are interconnected and interdependent.

Just like a flower, a human being does not exist independently. *You* don't exist independently. Not only are you connected to your parents, friends and relatives, but anything you do at any time in your day is dependent on other people's existence.

When you turn on the light in the morning. When you get dressed. When you eat. When you drive. When you use your phone. When you work. When you throw away rubbish. All your daily activities bind you into a web of interconnectedness with the rest of the human and non-human world, past, present and future.

How amazing is that?

49   A single garment of identity

In his commencement address for Oberlin College in June 1965, Dr Martin Luther King Jr pointed out that all human beings are connected to each other and all life is related. We cannot get away from 'the network of mutuality'.

We are, he said, 'tied in a single garment of identity'. For him, this had profound ramifications. In particular, we cannot be what we should be until all people are what they should be. The conditions of our existence are affected by the conditions of everyone else's existence.

How is your life affected by others? How do you touch others' lives?

50   Where are you going?

The painting *Where do we come from? What are we? Where are we going?* by French Post-Impressionist artist Paul Gauguin calls out to us with its deep indigo and bright yellows.

I like to imagine that Gauguin depicted a typical day in the life of the Tahitian town where he stayed for many years. For me, this painting represents the interconnectedness of all life. From birth to old age, we are embedded in relationships that make us who we are.

As an exercise, write about the people who make you who you are: parents, siblings, friends, teachers, mentors, colleagues, spiritual leaders, artists. Describe how they have contributed to who you are today.

Reflect on the interdependence that it highlights.

51   Where does your coffee come from (or your tea, or bananas)?

When his son questioned his dinner gratitude practice, the author A. A. Jacobs went on a quest to meet and personally thank every single person who had contributed to his morning cup of coffee. Yes, every single person!

Not only did he meet and thank the barista who handed him his coffee every morning, but also the person who designed the logo for the coffee brand, the truck driver who delivered the coffee beans, the woman in charge of pest control for the warehouse where the coffee beans were stored, and the farmers who grew the coffee in Colombia. I can't list every single person he thanked here, but you get the idea.

Obviously, we can't all go around the world thanking everyone who helps us live our life comfortably and pleasurably, but remembering every so often all the things that go into your daily life may help you realize how interdependent everything is and how you are connected with the wider world.

52   You are a lotus

Imagine you are a lotus on a serene pond. Imagine that at the centre of your petals sits a fully awakened buddha. This is what the Buddha said: all beings are like lotuses with a fully awakened buddha within them.

In time, this image developed into the idea that all beings have buddha-nature, a seed of buddhahood within them: human and non-human animals – yes, even that scary spider – all have buddha-nature.

We all have seeds of compassion and wisdom within us, and we can choose to water these seeds every day by acting kindly, generously and compassionately towards ourselves and towards others.

How will you water your buddha seed? How will you help it grow?

53   Why should I fear death?

The entire cosmos is a cooperative. The sun, the moon and the stars live together as a cooperative. The same is true for humans and animals, trees and soil. Our bodily parts function as a cooperative. When we realize that the world is a mutual, interdependent, cooperative enterprise, that human beings are all mutual friends in the process of birth, old age, suffering and death, then we can build a noble, even heavenly environment.

Ven. Bhikkhu Buddhadasa (1906–1993)

54   Living an engaged life: Thich Nhat Hanh

Zen master Thich Nhat Hanh (1926–2022) saw no separation between leading a spiritual life and being actively engaged in making the world a better place. His life showed that social activism was as much a part of Buddhism as meditation.

Thây (teacher in Vietnamese), as his students called him, was born in Vietnam and became a monk at 23. He became involved in peace activism early on and visited the US several times. There he met with religious leaders and social activists such as Thomas Merton and Dr Martin Luther King Jr to urge them to oppose the war in Vietnam. His fierce anti-war stance caused the Vietnamese government to bar him from returning to Vietnam, and he was granted asylum in France, where he founded Plum Village, an international monastic community and retreat center in the Zen tradition.

Over the following 60 years, Thich Nhat Hanh deeply influenced Western Buddhism. With 'engaged Buddhism' he brought social, political and environmental concerns to the fore of spiritual practice. He drew specifically on what he called 'interbeing' – the Buddhist principle of dependent origination that explains the interdependence of all things – and mindfulness, which, thanks in great part to his teachings, has now become mainstream in the West.

For him, being a Buddhist meant to actively seek to make the world a better place.

55   Develop your wisdom

How wise are you? One wisdom practice in Buddhist meditation is to acknowledge the impermanent nature of all things. The point is not to feel sad and maudlin. On the contrary. When we realize that, one day, our child's small hand will be a hand larger than ours, our parent's smile will only be a memory and that, eventually, all of us who live now will be no more than dust, we can better appreciate the stunning reality that we are alive now.

56   This tree is a monk (or a nun)

In Thailand, since the 1980s, monks have been ordaining trees as monks. They go to forests whose existence is threatened by extensive and unsustainable logging and they perform ordination ceremonies for trees by tying orange monastic robes around the trees' trunks. Local dignitaries and people attend – sometimes even celebrities turn up, as in 2010 when the Miss Universe Thailand contestants participated in one of the sylvan ordinations.

In showing their support for this unusual ritual, Thai people affirm their interdependence with the forest and claim that 'to harm the forest is to harm life'. Deforestation in Thailand (and in the world generally) has a more acute impact on the people who live near the forests, but it also has a global impact on climate change, desertification and the destruction of natural habitats.

By ordaining the trees as monks, in a country where monks have a sacred status, they are asserting the sacredness of the non-human world and embracing it under the protection of the Buddhist monastic community.

How do you embrace and protect the non-human world in your community?

57 Make the world a better place

Engaged Buddhism takes many different forms. For some, like many followers of Thich Nhat Hanh, it means going on long peace marches throughout Europe. For some, it's volunteering at the local soup kitchen. For others, it is being involved in politics. For yet others, it's doing their job in the best way they can, or caring for their loved ones.

What matters, says Thich Nhat Hanh, is that we recognize the interconnectedness of all life and seek to make the world a better place.

As an exercise, reflect on your contribution. Describe how and when, how often and with whom, what you do or would like to do to make the world a better place.

58 Life is change

We are often afraid of change and, of course, we are most fearful of the biggest change of all – death. But, without change, there is no life. Life is change. A seed sprouts and becomes a flower. The flower blooms and wilts. Her seeds are scattered. And the cycle starts again. A baby becomes a toddler who blooms into a child, a teenager and an adult. The cycle continues.

If the seed did not sprout, there would be no flower.

We may or may not have ideas about what occurs after death, but, without death, there is no life. Recognizing and accepting this truth is awakening to the true nature of things.

59   Are you walking your talk?

Our daily activities are an accurate reflection of our most deeply held values. I invite you to keep track of your daily activities for a day or a week or a month and to evaluate how truly they express your values.

For example, if you are concerned about the welfare of non-human animals, spending an hour checking your social media for cute videos of kittens may be consistent with your values but won't rate as high as volunteering your Saturdays at the local shelter for strays, donating to an animal welfare organization, or even just taking good care of your own pets.

Write down what you do on a day-to-day basis. The goal is not to be critical but to note where you can act to better match your actions with your values.

How do you feel about walking your talk?

60   What is the sound of one hand clapping?

'What is the sound of one hand clapping?' is a famous *kôan*. In Chan (Zen) Buddhism, a *kôan* is a paradoxical or absurd story that cannot be understood discursively or intellectually and is intended to cut through ordinary and conventional ways of thinking and reveal the true nature of reality.

Many Zen Buddhists receive a *kôan* from their teacher and spend years contemplating it in pursuit of this sudden awakening. In everyday terms, it is comparable to the 'aha' moment you have when, faced with a complicated situation or concept, you suddenly understand it without thinking it through step by step. It is a moment when you reach the deep source of your inner wisdom.

What *kôan* has life given you? When have you had sudden insights?

CHAPTER 3
KARMA (ACTION)

61   What is *karma*?

You've probably heard the term *karma* before. In the original languages of Buddhism, Pāli and Sanskrit, *karma* means action.

In Buddhism, *karma* is a morally relevant action and as such it originates in the mind as intention, which can be positive or negative. The moral quality of our intention has positive or negative consequences for us in the more or less immediate future.

The crucial aspect of the concept of *karma* is that it implies that we have agency: whatever the circumstances, in every instant, we choose to act out of positive or negative intentions.

62   What is your *karma*?

How does *karma* play out in your life? Even if you don't accept the Buddhist concept, you can play along since all actions have consequences whether you believe in *karma* or not.

Describe an action you performed in the past and the consequences it has had on you in the present. What motivations accompanied that action? Can you dig deep and describe the different (even contradictory) reasons that pushed you to engage in the action? What immediate results did it have? What longer-term results are you still experiencing today?

What reflections arise out of understanding the impact of this action on your life?

63   Taking the time for reflection

In Thailand, it is customary for young men to be ordained temporarily as monks. This rite of passage marks the transition from childhood to adulthood. The day of ordination is a festive occasion during which, usually, a whole group of men of similar age are ordained at the same time.

The event is a re-enactment of the Buddha's act of renunciation. The young men dress in 'royal' garb and arrive to great pomp, surrounded by a large group of relatives and friends. They formally ask permission from their parents to be ordained. Once the permission is given, their head and eyebrows are shaved and they change into monastic robes.

Often, the men take vows for the benefit of their mother or a sick parent or relative as it is believed that the merit of this good action can be transferred to the benefit of another person. After their time as monks, young men are considered ready for the responsibilities of adulthood. For those who are ordained as older men, monkhood is a time of reflection and contemplation during which they strengthen and renew their spiritual commitment.

In your life, what time do you devote to reflection and contemplation?

64   Root your actions in wisdom

French philosopher Pierre Hadot (1922–2010), in his book *The Present Alone is Our Happiness*, explains that reading ancient philosophy may seem irrelevant in today's world, especially as the ancient thinkers lived in such a different environment. Yet reading philosophy, religious texts and even poetry and fiction can illuminate certain contemporary ideas and concepts and also 'inspire an actual attitude in us, an inner act, or a spiritual exercise'.

Reading religious texts, philosophy, poetry, fiction or other inspiring texts gives us access to sources of wisdom and can help us reflect on our life as well as act in more mindful ways.

What are your sources of wisdom? How do you keep them in mind? Practise reading regularly, maybe even daily, and reflecting on the themes evoked in your readings.

65 Construct your reality

An important aspect of the Buddhist concept of *karma* is the notion that we are constantly constructing our reality out of our actions and reactions to the environment and the circumstances within which we find ourselves.

Constructing our reality also means that we are constructing who we are as human beings, because in a very fundamental way we are what we do. Someone who typically acts generously is a generous person. Someone who typically treats others with kindness is kind.

Be more mindful of the motivations of your actions (and reactions) to create a reality and a life that corresponds with who you want to be.

66 Intention is action

It is intention that I call action. Intending, you act by body, speech and mind.

The Buddha, *Anguttara Nikāya*, III, 415

67 Non-acting is acting

Western culture is very focused on action, efficiency and productivity. Mindfulness focuses on simply being present without acting, without seeking to produce anything at all, not even wellbeing, calm or mindfulness itself.

Sense perceptions come and go. Physical sensations come and go. Emotions come and go. Thoughts come and go. Intentions come and go. The urge to scratch your nose arises. Your stomach grumbles for hunger. Boredom arises. The urge to get up and do something more entertaining ensues. Thoughts of food surge. Plans develop.

Mindfulness does not reject, grasp or judge. Mindfulness takes it all in as the sky takes in clouds and birds, thunder and rain, planes and balloons, without judgement.

Abandon the urge to act on your every whim and desire, and put your energy and efforts where you really want them to be.

68   Transform your actions

The Buddhist path fundamentally aims to transform our actions by changing how we understand the world and our place in it. Buddhists aim to make their actions consistent with the three Buddhist virtues of kindness, generosity and wisdom.

Obviously, you don't have to be Buddhist to endeavour to act with kindness, generosity and wisdom. Importantly, you also don't have to be Buddhist to use and practise Buddhist mindfulness techniques to identify your values and transform your actions in ways that reflect those values.

69   Forgive yourself

Buddhist monks and nuns recite the monastic rules and confess their offences in a fortnightly communal ceremony. This allows them to 'purify' their actions, so to speak, and to start each fortnight anew.

With this exercise, I encourage you to purify your actions by writing about an action (or omission) you feel regret or guilt about. This is just for you. You need not share it with anyone and may destroy it as soon as you have finished writing.

This kind of writing exercise has been shown to help release guilt or regret. Include as many details as possible: When was it? Where? And with whom? What emotions were present at the time? What emotions are present now? Why do you regret the action or omission? What impact did it have on you? On others?

Once you have finished writing, consider whether you are ready to forgive yourself, and if you are, write this down too.

70   Waves on the ocean: the teachings of Machig Labdrön

Legend has it that Machig Labdrön (1055–1149) was special from the moment of her birth. She was able to speak as soon as she was born and could read by the time she was five. By the time she was 13, she could recite the 8,000 verses of the *Perfection of Wisdom*, one of the key philosophical Mahāyāna Buddhist texts on emptiness, eight times a day.

Machig was born in Tibet, south-east of Lhasa, the daughter of a village chief, at a time when very few people, let alone girls, learned how to read. Her ability to recite the sacred texts allowed her to study at a monastery with a renowned teacher and to continue learning sacred texts and meditation practices from several masters. In time, she composed her own philosophical texts and expanded the meditative practice of Chöd, which seeks to cut through dualistic thinking.

According to Machig Labdrön, our dualistic tendency to categorize all things as good or bad causes our suffering. When we abandon discrimination between positive and negative and see all thoughts as 'waves on the ocean', we are released from attachment and can rest in the clear and luminous nature of the mind.

71   Put it on your schedule

Most of us have plans and projects. Some of them are imposed on us – our job, our family, our personal circumstances. Others are self-imposed. We also have secret aspirations.

For example, we secretly want to sing in a musical, or paint watercolours, or change career, or volunteer for an organization whose work we admire. Often, we put these aside for 'when we have time'. Only, Oliver Burkeman reminds us in his book *Four Thousand Weeks: Time Management for Mortals*, time never magically appears out of nowhere. He recommends scheduling time for these secret aspirations.

Put it on your calendar, once a day, once a week, or even just once a month. *Make* the time for it if it is important for you. That's the only way you will be able to *find* the time.

72   Your personal *nirvāṇa*

In Buddhist thought, there are two main kinds of actions: skilful and unskilful. Actions are skilful when they are motivated by the three positive roots of kindness, generosity and wisdom. They are unskilful when they are motivated by the three negative roots of hatred, greed and ignorance.

When we act skilfully, we get closer to *nirvāṇa*. When we act unskilfully, we move away from it.

To speak in more secular terms, actions are performed to achieve specific goals, and for most of us, through these goals, we aim to reach a certain level of happiness or contentment with our life.

Think about this happiness or contentment as your personal *nirvāṇa*. Any action you take will either get you closer to this personal *nirvāṇa* or it won't. When it does, it's skilful. When it doesn't, it's unskilful.

Are your actions skilful or unskilful? Do they take you closer to your personal *nirvāṇa*?

73   A habit for life

From a simple psychological perspective, every time we engage in an action, we strengthen synaptic connections and therefore become more likely to engage in the same type of action in the future. This is how we create habits, and this is also how we change habits.

Some say that it is enough to do something for three weeks to create a habit, others that you need nearly a year. Whatever the case may be, it is certain that the more we do something, the more likely we are to do it, and that the 'doing it' becomes easier the longer we do it. Buddhist psychology even explains that habits continue from life to life as tendencies to engage in some behaviours and not others.

What habit will you develop? How long will you stick with it to start?

74   Without hope of reward

Without hope of reward
Provide help to others
Bear suffering alone
And share your pleasures with beggars.

Nāgārjuna, *Ratnāvāli*, 169

75   Show yourself you can

This is a simple challenge. Choose something that you've been wanting to do for a long time but have never got round to. Be clear and specific about what it is.

For example, exercise three times a week. Eat green vegetables or fruit daily. Journal. Call friends and relatives regularly. Maybe it is work-related. Or maybe you really want to learn salsa dancing. Whatever it is, be sure to have a clear idea. Decide when, where and how often you will do it.

And now, do it, FOR A MONTH. Without fail.

Make a commitment to yourself that you will not end the day without performing your habit. This means you might be eating your spinach just before heading to bed, or trying to do that tricky salsa step at two minutes before midnight. Keep a log so that you can tick off each day and see the streak building up.

Hold yourself to it, just to show yourself you can.

76 What is your stupa?

In Buddhist countries, shrines containing relics are found everywhere – these shrines are called *stupas*.

In one of the Pāli discourses, the Buddha enjoined his followers to share his relics after his death and enshrine them in *stupas* built at crossroads so that when people come across them, they may be reminded of his teachings and be filled with joy and serenity. Devotees make offerings of flowers, incense and candles at these *stupas* and often circumambulate them while reciting prayers and mantras.

These activities serve to calm the mind and to remember the Buddhist virtues. What is *your stupa*? Identify an object or a place that can serve as a reminder to settle your mind and remember the virtues you want to embody.

77 Do you have a system?

Life in Buddhist monasteries is highly regulated, even in its smallest aspects such as the proper way to chew food, wear monastic garments or walk around the temple. The monastic rules are called the *pātimokkha*, and Buddhist monks and nuns hold each other responsible for following them.

According to James Clear, the renowned habit specialist, to achieve our goals, it is more important to design an effective system than to spend much time on designing the goals themselves. An effective system allows us to develop habits that become who we are over time and support our goals.

We can see such a system at work in the Buddhist monastic rules. By observing them and holding each other accountable, monks and nuns not only observe proper behaviour but also progress towards their goal of awakening (*nirvāṇa*).

You may not need rules for how you chew your food, but you can devise daily routines that can serve as the foundation for a system to help you progress towards your goals.

78   Choose a habit

When you are mindful of why you want to develop certain habits, you are more likely to stick with them. What habits would you like to develop?

Make a list and pick the top two or three. Explain why you want to develop these habits. What benefits will they bring you? Describe the habits in detail, what they entail and how, when and where you can perform them. Think about the obstacles you will surely encounter and how to address them.

Once you have done this exercise, pick one habit and write down when and where you will start implementing it and for how long.

79   Give up action

Train yourself in this practice. Next time you are about to act on impulse, whether it's buying something you don't actually need, or eating something you know is not good for you, or opening a social media app, stop yourself. Just don't do it.

Breathe deeply. Remind yourself you're practising giving up action. If the urge is very strong, sit down or stand up, breathe three long breaths. Feel the air expanding your lungs and your belly, or feel your chest rising. Examine the urge: Where is it in your body? How does it feel? Breathe deeply. Don't reject the urge. Welcome it. Ask it what it is trying to tell you.

Remember, don't act on it because, right now, you're practising giving up action.

80   Heirs to their actions

In the *Majjhima Nikāya*, the Buddha says that 'beings are heirs to their actions'. What does he mean by that? At the most basic level, we are what we do, and the more we do something, the more we are prone to do it; therefore an action shapes the future actions we will take.

In addition, when we perform an action, we set in motion a chain of events over which we may have little or no control but which will still affect us.

Finally, more likely than not, we will bear the consequences of our actions in a more or less distant future. Either our actions will affect our life circumstances or they will affect how we feel.

In other words, the Buddha is encouraging us to be more mindful about the consequences of our actions.

81   An act of kindness

No act of kindness, no matter how small, is ever wasted.

Aesop, The Lion and the Mouse,

82   Do nothing

In a chapter entitled 'Action', this is your chance to do NOTHING! Yes, do nothing. Don't scroll on your phone, don't read, don't do the dishes, don't even meditate. Just sit there and do nothing.

This is how you can practise the habit of doing nothing: once a day, put your phone on flight mode, set a timer for a minute or two, sit there and do nothing.

Be very sure to do nothing: do not use this time to think about a problem or plan your dinner. Actively do nothing. Look around you. Or gaze out of the window. What's there? What does it look like? What colours, what shapes can you see? What sounds can you hear? What sensations can you feel?

That's it! Your time's up. You can go back to doing something.

83 Body, speech and mind

Buddhist psychology classifies all actions into three categories: body, speech and mind. It's easy to understand that there are actions of body and speech, but in a Western context, thinking is not usually considered an action.

In the Buddhist context, however, thought is an action when an intention is present. For example, being hungry (although it occurs in the mind as well as in the body) is not an action. But thinking 'I will eat lunch in an hour' is an action – albeit a rather neutral one.

Why does it matter that thoughts motivated by intentions are considered to be actions? According to Buddhist psychology, it matters because all actions have consequences and our thoughts and intentions create our experience. It is more likely that you will eat lunch in an hour if you have set your intention to do so than if you have not.

It tells you that, amazingly, you have more control than you think: you can shape your experience by shaping your thoughts and intentions in ways that agree with your goals.

84 Break a habit

Mindfulness demands that we be aware of our intentions. Unfortunately, we often engage in mindless activities and develop habits we are dissatisfied with.

What are the habits you would like to change? Choose one or two and describe what the habit is. How often do you engage in it? What impact does it have on you and others around you?

Describe why you want to break it. What beneficial impact will it have on you and others? How will you go about breaking it?

Research has shown that replacing an unhelpful habit with a positive habit is more likely to succeed. Describe what positive habit you will develop to replace the one you want to break.

85 Act on your principles: Janice Willis

In her book *Dharma Matters: Women, Race, and Tantra*, African American Buddhist Janice (Jan) Willis doesn't mince her words: she calls out to American Buddhists to act on their principles of equanimity and compassion for all and to become more inclusive.

Jan Willis was born in 1948, and her childhood in the American South was marked by hate crimes. She has been teaching Buddhism both as a scholar at Wesleyan University since 1977 and since 1969 as a practitioner studying with the Tibetan teacher Lama Thubten Yeshe, whom she met in Nepal when she travelled there as a college student.

For Jan, Lama Yeshe's teachings on deity yoga, the visualization of oneself as a buddha, is a powerful instrument of self-transformation for all, and for African Americans in particular, because it instils confidence in one's own perfect nature. She believes that making American Buddhism more inclusive will not only benefit those, like African Americans, who have been marginalized, but will make Buddhism itself more vibrant and authentic.

86 Consider these questions

Be mindful of your actions. Ask yourself, before you take a course of action or make a commitment: Is this action or commitment something the person I want to be would support and approve of? Is this an action or commitment I am proud of now and that my future self will be proud of?

Remind yourself to consider these questions as a mindfulness practice.

87   Mind the gap

In a fundamental way, mindfulness seeks to create a gap between a stressor and the stress response. Our bodies and minds have evolved to respond to imminent threats (such as lions or wolves) in three basic ways: the 'flight, fight or freeze' response. But we seldom encounter lions or wolves on our way to the supermarket.

When we get cut up on the road, or bumped into on the subway, or when our boss criticizes us, or even when we self-criticize, we experience a stress response that is usually disproportionate to the actual threat.

Because we encounter many low-level external and internal stressors throughout the day, we maintain a low level of stress that, research has shown, adversely impacts our mental and physical health.

Mindfulness meditation offers a means to interrupt this unhealthy cycle by turning our attention to the physical sensations of stress and strengthening our ability to observe them as physical sensations. The more you develop mindfulness, the more you are able to let stress arise and dissipate.

88   Wash your bowl!

A Zen story says that one day a young monk, who had just entered the monastery, asked Master Jōshū (778–897) to give him some instructions. Master Jōshū replied, 'Have you had breakfast?'

When the young man said he had, Jōshū told him, 'Go and wash your bowl now.'

Sometimes we need to do what is there to do rather than getting lost in conjectures, planning or rumination.

Where, in your life, do you need to just go and wash your bowl?

89   Examine your motivations

We might think that we have a clear idea of our motivations for doing or not doing the things we do. If that were the case, psychoanalysts and psychotherapists would soon be out of work!

Examining our motivations more carefully and intentionally is possible and useful. For example, let's say you just agreed to an inconvenient request from a friend. What was your motivation? Did you really want to help? Or were you concerned about upsetting your friend if you refused? Or, say, you shouted at your partner or your child. Were you angry at them for their action right there, right then? Or are there other underlying reasons that motivated your anger?

In this way, you can cultivate the habit of reflecting on your motivation.

90   Get rid of FOMO!

Get rid of FOMO! Take at least three sheets of paper (not your journal or a digital device). List everything you want to do and never find the time to – the books or magazines you want to read, the places you want to visit, the hobbies you want to pick up, the friends you want to call but never do, the trendy diets or workouts you want to try, the films or TV shows you want to watch, the good habits you want to acquire, the bad habits you want to lose – your imagination is the limit.

Now, consider each carefully and ask yourself how crucial it is to you. If it is, write it on a new sheet of paper, then go on to the next one and ask yourself the same question. When you have finished the first list, get rid of it. Yes! Burn it, put it in the bin or shred it and eat it (just joking!).

Now, move on to the second (ideally much shorter) list and go through the same process, but this time ask yourself what you have time for, realistically, at this point in your life. If the item passes muster, write it on a third sheet of paper. Choose carefully as you should add no more than three items on this third list.

Get rid of the second list, no regrets, no fear of missing out. Now you have time to focus on these three things you really want to do.

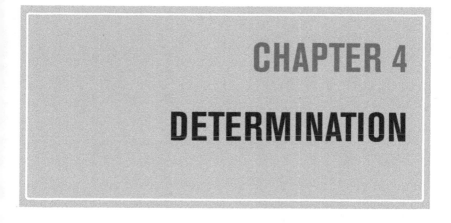

CHAPTER 4

DETERMINATION

91   The perfection of determination

Determination is one of the ten perfections of the Buddhist path, the qualities that the Buddha is said to have perfected during many lifetimes and that, by extension, Buddhists aim to develop in their daily life.

Determination is the quality that follows intention and is necessary to achieve any goal. If intention is the spark that gets us started, determination is the fuel that propels us and helps us persevere when the rush and excitement of novelty have waned and we are confronted with the routine of repetition.

Buddhist texts describe three qualities of determination: stamina, persistence and effort. By cultivating these qualities, you strengthen the determination to achieve your goals.

92   Is it conducive to the goal?

The Buddha often told his followers to consider whether a practice or action was conducive to the realization of the path.

What do you aspire to? Describe some of your aspirations and what they mean to you. Write about the daily actions that will help you realize them in your life.

What can you realistically start implementing right now? Keep in mind the question: 'How is it conducive to my goal?'

93   The undeterred resolve of Mahāpajāpatī

According to Buddhist tradition, Mahāpajāpatī was the Buddha's aunt and stepmother. She was also his milk-mother because she nourished him when his mother (her sister and co-wife to King Suddhodana, the Buddha's father) died seven days after his birth.

Mahāpajāpatī is best known as the founder of the Buddhist nuns' order. Buddhist texts recount that she was so determined to obtain the Buddha's permission to establish a Buddhist nuns' lineage that, after he first refused, she cut off her long hair, discarded her royal garments and put on the monastic ochre robes. She then walked from the royal capital, Kapilavatthu, to Vesali, a city more than 300 kilometres (185 miles) away.

When she arrived, her feet swollen and her robes dusty from the many days of walking, she waited outside the hall where the Buddha was staying. Ānanda, the Buddha's attendant, asked her why she was in such a dishevelled and dejected state, and upon learning about what had occurred, he decided to intercede in her favour.

He cleverly reminded the Buddha that it was he, the Buddha, who had proclaimed that women's spiritual capacity to attain awakening was equal to that of men. He also added that Mahāpajāpatī had kindly cared for the Buddha when he was an infant, feeding him with her own milk.

The Buddha finally relented and accepted that Mahāpajāpatī should be ordained, rewarding her determination with the realization of her goal. Mahāpajāpatī went on to lead the community of nuns with compassion and wisdom for many years until her death.

94   Don't let the tracking be the point

I was recently relieved to hear that I am not the only one who does something not because I really want to, or even have time to, but simply to keep the streak going – like walking my last thousand steps at 11:45 at night. On a podcast with philosopher C. Thi Nguyen, the journalist Ezra Klein pretty much admitted that he keeps meditating because his streak is so long, he cannot imagine breaking it.

C. Thi Nguyen's work on the gamification of life shows that when we become more concerned about the streak (or the points, such as in school grades, or money, such as when we monetize a hobby) than the activity itself, we end up losing the pleasure and enjoyment of doing something for its own sake. We also discount, to our detriment, the non-quantifiable aspects of the activity – such as inspiration, creativity or appreciation.

Once in a while, don't measure! Let go of that tracking device. Don't tick your habit calendar. Do something for its own sake. Just immerse yourself in the doing of it.

95   The four determinations

The four determinations:
One should not neglect discernment,
And should mind the truth,
One should aim to let go,
and train only for calm.

The Buddha, *Majjhima Nikāya*, 140

96   A finely tuned instrument

In a sutta, the Buddha addresses Sona, one of his monks, who is feeling disheartened because he has not yet attained *nirvāṇa*, the highest Buddhist realization, even though he has been practising walking meditation until the sole of his feet bled – all to no avail.

Aware that Sona played the lute before being ordained as a monk, the Buddha compares his efforts to the tuning of his lute. He explains that if the strings are too tight or too loose, the lute cannot be played: the strings must be at exactly the right tension for the pitch to be true. Similarly, if Sona is too tense, he becomes restless and scattered. If he is too slack, he will feel sleepy and unmotivated. Either way, he cannot achieve his goal. He must pitch his efforts at exactly the right level to attain *nirvāṇa*.

The Buddha's advice to Sona includes five qualities that can apply to any goal you determine to pursue: the conviction that the goal is worthy, persistence, mindfulness of the quality of your efforts, concentration, and the discernment that your efforts are effective.

How can you apply these to your own goals?

97   In what direction will you go?

According to the principle of *karma*, every decision you make will impact your future life (Buddhists actually say that there will be consequences in future lives also, but let's stay with this one life for now).

For every decision, you have a choice: you can take the easy road and do whatever requires the least effort, or you can choose to act in a way consistent with the kind of person you want to be. Every instant provides the opportunity to make this choice.

Develop the habit of asking yourself: 'Will this action take me in the direction I want to go?'

98   The admirable friend

In the *Upaḍḍha Sutta*, the Buddha declares that the whole of the spiritual life consists in admirable friendship (*kalyāṇamittatā*) and offers himself as an admirable friend to all beings.

Because one who follows admirable friends is better able to develop the qualities of the Noble Eightfold Path, later commentators have usually considered as admirable friends the monks and nuns who, ideally, seek to cultivate the Seven Qualities of Awakening and serve as teachers to the lay community. In Tibetan Buddhism, the idea of the admirable friend culminates in the *guru*, the teacher who guides the disciple all the way to full awakening.

In contemporary Western Buddhism, the admirable friendship is more commonly understood as spiritual friendship between peers on the spiritual path. They serve as role models to each other and provide mutual encouragement and support.

What about you? In what ways are you an admirable friend?

99 Milarepa's advice to Gampopa

When Milarepa (1040–1123) became Marpa Lotsawa's disciple, he had to demonstrate his great determination. Marpa treated Milarepa harshly, imposing hard labour and many penances on him. Most famously, Marpa made him build stone towers with his bare hands, only to have him demolish them again. Eventually, Milarepa's efforts paid off and Marpa finally agreed to teach him the Dharma (the Buddhist teachings).

Milarepa became an accomplished yogi who spent years meditating in a cave and, legend says, eating nettles for food, to the point that his skin became green. He was willing to face hardships and privations to attain awakening, but his most memorable teaching is the one he gave Gampopa (1079–1153), one of his main disciples and the founder of the Kagyu tradition, one of the four main Tibetan Buddhist schools.

After years of training him, Milarepa saw that Gampopa was ready to be sent back to his monastery. As Gampopa walked away, Milarepa called him back and, showing him his buttocks covered in calluses from decades of sitting in meditation, shouted, 'This is the most important teaching, Gampopa, practise!'

100 Who are your admirable friends?

Modern social psychology shows that the ancient Buddhist idea of 'admirable friend' (kalyāṇamitta) is rooted in social dynamics: we are strongly influenced by our close friendships in good (and bad) ways. Surrounding yourself with people who elicit the best in you can have a lasting positive impact on your wellbeing.

Take a moment to think about your close relationships and what they bring you. Write about your close friends: What do you like and enjoy about them? Which of their qualities do you admire and want to emulate? Who gives you a shoulder to lean on, or a nudge to prod you forward? In which ways do your friends encourage and support you in being the best 'you' you can be? Which friendships do you want to sustain and which do you want to turn away from?

101 Defeat the hindrances!

We all face daily obstacles when it comes to implementing our goals or being disciplined. Sometimes these obstacles are external and cannot be controlled. Often, however, the obstacle is our resistance to doing what needs to be done, the natural and universal tendency to conserve energy as one of my friends puts it, or the Five Hindrances, in Buddhist terms.

One practice to deal with the hindrances is to remind yourself of the values that underlie your goals. Once you clearly connect your goals and values with your daily actions, you will be more energized and motivated.

Remind yourself also that acting in a way consistent with your values might feel burdensome right now, but it will always feel deeply fulfilling and rewarding afterwards.

102 Great faith, great doubt, great determination

Three qualities are considered paramount in Zen Buddhism: great faith, great doubt and great determination.

Great faith is the conviction that everyone is capable of reaching awakening. Everyone, including you and me, already has within them the seeds of goodness and wisdom.

Great doubt is the capacity to question our deeply held beliefs, prejudices and preconceptions, especially those we have never questioned before. Most importantly, great doubt requires us to continue questioning whenever we think that we have attained any sort of realization. In a profound way, it is letting go of certainty and allowing uncertainty in our lives.

Finally, *great determination* is, at its most basic, the capacity to persevere regardless of the circumstances.

Taken together, these three great qualities help us pursue valued goals, trusting that we will succeed while remaining flexible and responsive, even as we are relentless in our pursuit.

103   As a mountain...

As a mountain, stable and firmly based, does not tremble in rough
winds but remains in precisely its own place, so you too must
be constantly stable in resolute determination; going on to the
perfection of determination, you will attain awakening.

The Buddha, *Buddhavamsa*, II, 154–5

104   Find a stick

In Japanese Zen meditation halls, a meditation monitor walks between the meditators who are facing the wall for their meditation. When a meditator shows signs of losing concentration or falls asleep, the monitor gently calls their attention. The meditator bows respectfully and shifts slightly so that the monitor can strike them with a wooden stick on the meaty part of the shoulders.

We all lose concentration and get distracted, especially when we are on our digital devices. What is the stick that brings you back to the present? If you don't have one, think about what you could use: A timer? A monitoring app? Whatever it is, find your stick.

105   Your commitment

One implication of *karma* – the Buddhist concept that our actions have consequences – is that the more we do something, the more we are likely to do it.

Your challenge today is to choose an activity you have been wanting to pursue more regularly and make a plan. Choose a time when you know you can do it and commit to doing it every day at that time for two minutes for a month. Every single day for two minutes at the same time – not one minute, not three minutes, just two minutes.

At the end of the month, you can increase the duration of the activity, but you must commit to continuing to do it for another month at this new duration; otherwise, keep it at two minutes.

For example, if you want to read more, commit to reading for two minutes at 7 p.m. every day. If it's exercising, commit to doing push-ups or planks or squats, or yoga, or weight lifting for two minutes at 6 a.m. each day.

Your choice, your commitment.

106   Simplicity

Our life is frittered away by detail. Simplicity, simplicity, simplicity. I say, let your affairs be as two or three, and not a hundred or a thousand.

David Henry Thoreau (1817–1862)

107   Which one do you pick?

Not everyone desires to give up worldly life and become a monk or a nun, or to meditate for years in a cave in the Himalayas. Some of us want to meditate just a bit and carry on with our families and jobs.

Buddhism acknowledges these differences in aspiration by describing the spiritual path in various ways that are, in some sense, tailored to individual needs. When taking into account the traditions, sub-traditions, schools and sub-schools of Buddhism, there exists a plethora of practices to choose from. Some are as easy as lighting incense and making offerings to the Buddha while others involve complex ritual practices that require years of study.

A practice like mindfulness is also done outside of religious contexts. When you find one that best suits your aspiration and temperament, you are much more likely to persevere and be successful. Which one do you pick?

108   Discover 'foop'

Sometimes we are in difficult situations, whether at work or in a relationship. We swing from wanting to make it work to flailing in despair that we just can't.

The Nagoski sisters, in their book *Burnout: The Secret to Unlocking the Stress Cycle*, evocatively coined a new word for this feeling of being stuck in this back and forth between diametrically opposed desires: 'foop'.

When we are mired in 'foop', they advise us to develop a mindful attitude by answering two sets of questions to determine the best short- and long-term options: What are the benefits and costs of continuing? And what are the benefits and costs of stopping? Aim to be honest with yourself when answering these questions to reach greater clarity.

109   Sweep the floor

Cūḷapanthaka, in the *Theragātha*, recounts how he was tormented by his brother Mahāpanthaka, also a monk, because he could not remember the intricacies of the Buddha's teachings.

One time, the story goes, Mahāpanthaka went too far: he told Cūḷapanthaka that he would never be able to attain awakening because he was too dull and that he should just leave the monastery. Cūḷapanthaka, distraught, burst into tears just as the Buddha approached. When Cūḷapanthaka explained to him what Mahāpanthaka said, the Buddha reassured him that by following his advice he would certainly become awakened. He walked the monk to his cell and handing him a broom said, 'Cūḷapanthaka, every day sweep this ground and think, "I sweep impurity."'

Cūḷapanthaka followed the Buddha's advice and swept the floor day after day, repeating 'I sweep impurity'. Slowly his mind opened until, finally, he reached awakening.

Like Cūḷapanthaka, you can do a small thing every day towards your awakening.

110   Don't wait to feel motivated

I find it is easy to have grand dreams and make plans, but when it's cold and still dark outside and the bed is warm and cosy, it's not easy to live up to my intentions. Motivation is not always waiting nearby to pull me out of bed. So, I just roll over and go back to sleep, only to feel miserable and frustrated later for my lack of determination.

The secret to getting out of bed, I have learned, is to act even when I am not motivated. Motivation comes and goes. We cannot depend on it. We must do what we have to do whether we feel like it or not.

This is what Oliver Burkeman, in his book *The Antidote: Happiness for People Who Can't Stand Positive Thinking*, points out. He explains that highly successful writers or artists all have in common a strict routine: they just did the same thing, at the same time, every single day, without fail. They didn't wait to feel motivated.

What kind of routine can you establish to live up to your intentions?

111   The bodhisattva vow

The bodhisattva vow is taken when someone decides they want to endeavour to become a Buddha. It is the vow that the Buddha of our time period, Gotama Buddha (called Śakyamūni Buddha in Mahāyāna Buddhism), made when he vowed to pursue buddhahood.

A bodhisattva is a being who is intent on awakening for the benefit of all. In early Buddhism, only a few extraordinary individuals were believed to have made this wish. With the rise of Mahāyāna Buddhism, the notion developed that the path of the bodhisattva was not restricted to just these few extraordinary individuals but instead that anyone can pursue it.

Many Mahāyāna practitioners recite the bodhisattva vow daily as a morning ritual. Repeating it is a reminder to which they return again and again to renew and strengthen their determination to put into practice the intention they proclaimed when they made their vow to act for the welfare of all beings.

What reminders help you follow through with your intentions?

112   Like leaves in a storm

One morning, I made my way to my teacher's empty sitting room. I planned to meditate, but my laudable purpose was not shared by disobedient thoughts. They scattered like birds before the hunter. 'Mukunda!' My teacher's voice sounded from a distant balcony.

I felt as rebellious as my thoughts. 'My teacher always urges me to meditate,' I muttered to myself. 'He should not disturb me when he knows why I came to his room.' He summoned me again; I remained obstinately silent. The third time his tone held rebuke. 'Sir, I am meditating,' I shouted in protest. 'I know how you are meditating,' my guru called out, 'with your mind scattered like leaves in a storm!'

Paramahansa Yogananda (1893–1952), *Autobiography of a Yogi*

113   What's stopping you?

Our determination is often thwarted by what Buddhist psychology calls the Five Hindrances – obstacles that prevent us from living up to our intentions.

While Buddhist texts are most concerned with meditative practices, the hindrances can arise in any context. You may be working towards a work or school project, or you may want to exercise or volunteer more consistently, but, like the meditator in her cave, you are assailed by a range of feelings and emotions. Sometimes you are hungry or bored, or outright angry with the demands placed on you. Other times you are tired or sleepy or, on the contrary, restless and worried. Finally, you start questioning the value of the task at hand.

These are the Five Hindrances: sensual desires, hostility, sleepiness, restlessness and doubt. Know them for what they are – feelings and thoughts that, like all things, arise, linger and dissipate.

Don't give them the power to stop you.

114   Check with your body

The eighteenth-century Japanese Zen master Hakuin Ekaku (1689–1769) was so determined to attain awakening that he practised meditation and extreme austerities for many years with no regard for his health.

When he was in his twenties, Hakuin fell ill with what he called meditation sickness. He sought the advice of the Daoist master Hakuyu, who recommended a visualization practice to strengthen his vital energy. From then on, Hakuin insisted on the importance of physical health and made it a part of his Zen practice.

In the modern world, we are all a bit like the young Hakuin and ignore our health until illness strikes. Make a practice to check with your body and attend to it regularly.

115   What are your hindrances?

The Five Hindrances in Buddhist meditation are the five obstacles to your meditative practice: sensual desires, hostility, sleepiness, restlessness and doubt. When you think about it, however, you can see that they are not specific to meditation but apply to all areas of life.

This means that we can use the same strategies that meditation teachers give to meditators to address the hindrances in their meditation to find ways to tackle hindrances in our daily life.

Write down some of the things you seek to accomplish and the obstacles you face in their realization. Describe strategies to deal with these obstacles so that next time the hindrances arise, you are well prepared.

116   Listen

Take a moment. Sit down. Set a timer if that helps you stay put – two minutes, three minutes … five minutes if you're feeling brave – but commit to continue until it goes off.

Close your eyes. Listen. What do you hear? Cars passing? Birds chirping? The wind blowing? Can you hear the swish of your clothes around you as you breathe deeply? The whisper of your breath entering your nostrils? The gurgles of your stomach? Can you hear the furniture and walls creaking? Machines whirring and purring? Can you hear life living softly?

Stay focused on the sounds outside and inside you. When your attention drifts away, gently bring it back to the sounds. What else can you hear?

117   Start small

Despite what people generally believe, Buddhists around the world don't always practise meditation daily, but they very often make an offering of food or incense to the Buddha image in their homes in the morning before setting out for their daily activities, a practice that can take as little as a minute or two. This way, they do something easy and quick every day to bring to mind the spiritual path, even when they don't have time or lack motivation.

This is not very different from what James Clear, author of the bestseller *Atomic Habits*, recommends we do to follow through with our intentions and cultivate determination. Because motivation fluctuates depending on circumstances, he suggests starting with something easy enough that it is possible to do it even when we don't feel motivated at all.

What habit do you want to cultivate? Think of something simple you can do every day to get started.

118   Happiness

Those only are happy who have their minds fixed on some object other than their own happiness; on the happiness of others, on the improvement of humankind, even on some art or pursuit, followed not as a means but as itself an ideal end. Aiming thus at something else, they find happiness by the way.

John Stuart Mill (1806–73), *Autobiography*

119   Embrace it all

Yale professor Laurie Santos, on her podcast *The Happiness Lab*, did a series on embracing negative emotions and developing the capacity to not only accept but to welcome them as an inevitable and valuable aspect of being human. Her guests argued that experiencing our negative emotions – anger, sadness, grief, anxiety and languishing – is the only way to live a full life and to wholly enjoy our positive emotions.

Just as we can't have day without night, or warmth without cold, we can't really appreciate our positive emotions if we don't acknowledge and consciously experience the negative ones.

Mindfulness practice encourages you to do exactly this: recognize your feelings and emotions just as they are, without judgement. Explore them with kind attention and interest. Experience how they feel in your body.

Embrace it all and release it all.

120   Call the earth to witness

The night the Buddha attained the ultimate spiritual realization, *nirvāṇa*, it is said that he was visited by Māra, who in Buddhist texts personifies all the evil and malicious tendencies of human nature – our dark side, so to speak.

Māra was aiming to disrupt the Buddha and prevent him from attaining his goal. He appeared as an army of men wielding terrifying weapons to frighten the Buddha into giving up. He appeared as a group of beautiful young women to seduce the Buddha and lead him astray.

All the while, the Buddha remained still, his hand touching the earth, calling it to witness his steadfastness and determination to attain *nirvāṇa*. Māra finally gave up his challenge and left, feeling miserable.

Whom or what do you call to witness to chase Māra away when you are being distracted from your goal?

CHAPTER 5

MINDFULNESS

121   A single moment

When the Buddha said to his followers that, if they could spend just one single moment fully present to their experience, they would attain awakening and liberation from suffering, he was referring to mindfulness.

Mindfulness consists in bringing your full attention to the present moment without any judgement or objective, besides being present to the moment.

What does it mean in practice? Focus on one specific thing. Traditionally, the focus is on the breath because it is a good anchor for attention since it is always present, but you can choose sounds, for example, or the sensations in your body.

As the mind wanders away, notice the wandering and bring it back to your anchor. Again. And again. There is nothing wrong with the mind wandering – that's the mind doing its thing. Thoughts, feelings, emotions and sensations arise. You notice them and you bring the mind back. Again. And again.

122   Scan your body

Try this meditation. Sit on a cushion, on a chair or lie down, but make sure you don't fall asleep. Keep your body straight and comfortable, your chin slightly tucked in and your hands either on your lap if you're sitting or at your sides or on your stomach if you're lying down. Close your eyes: this will help you to focus on the bodily sensations.

Start with three deep breaths, breathing in calm and relaxation and breathing out stress and worries. When you are ready, focus on the top of your head. Note any sensation at your scalp, your forehead, your cheeks, your mouth and the back of your head. Take your time as you do this and focus on experiencing the sensations as they are, without judgement.

Now observe your neck and your shoulders. Note any sensation. Is it tight or relaxed? Does it feel warm or cool? Any tingling or pulsing? Notice without judging. Continue the practice through your chest, stomach, arms, hands, legs and feet. For each, observe the sensations without judging them.

When you arrive at the feet, take a moment or two to enjoy being in your body. It is *your* body, and despite issues you think it might have, it does its best to serve you well. Thank it for that.

123   Why be mindful?

Why do you want to be mindful? What do you hope it will bring to your life right now? And in the future? What areas of your life do you want to develop mindfulness in?

Take a moment to write about these questions, and clarify for yourself what you hope mindfulness will bring to your life.

124   Mindfulness of the body and mind

In the *Foundations of Mindfulness Sutta*, the Buddha explains how to establish mindfulness of the body and mind. He starts with the breath, telling us to observe the breath as it rises and falls, noticing whether it is long or short, deep or shallow. He then tells us to contemplate the body as it is, with its limbs, muscles and organs, and to notice the sensations throughout, just as they are: pleasant, unpleasant or neutral.

He continues with the mind, urging us to observe thoughts, feelings and emotions, and to notice their quality: pleasant, unpleasant or neutral. Note that the evaluation of sensations, thoughts, emotions and feelings is non-judgemental – it consists in acknowledging that a sensation, a thought, an emotion or a feeling is present and is either pleasant, unpleasant or neutral. It does *not* consist in judging whether it is good or bad, whether you want it or not – just accept what is.

125   Before eating

Develop the habit of eating more mindfully. Put down this book or your digital device – after you have read this, of course!

Look at your plate. What is on it? Meat? Vegetables? Carbs? Did you prepare it yourself? If not, do you know who prepared it? Can you easily identify the ingredients? What shape does it have? What colour? What texture?

Now that you have observed its external appearance, bring it closer and smell its perfume. What does it smell of? Is it earthy? Fresh? Sharp? Fruity? Toasty? Does it smell of nature or of something more chemical or greasy?

Take your time and observe your food carefully. Think about what needs this food will fulfil for you: Will it bring you much-needed nutrients and energy? Or will it satisfy a craving? Simply make a note of it and how it makes you feel.

126   You're meditating!

In a busy life, it can be difficult, not to say impossible, to find time to meditate. But meditation does not have to be separate from life. In fact, it should not be.

The Vinaya, the monastic code, has precise rules for how Buddhist monks and nuns should deport themselves in daily activities such as eating, walking, bathing and even using the bathroom. The main point of these rules is not to be needlessly fastidious about how monks and nuns should chew their food or hold their arms while walking, but to bring mindfulness to every single aspect of their lives.

Try it for yourself. Bring mindfulness to everyday activities. Observe, without any judgement, how you eat, shower, brush your teeth. Be fully present in your body and your movements. You're meditating!

127 Watch your mind: Bhikkhunī Voramai's rule

When Venerable Bhikkhunī Voramai was born as Lamai Kabilsingh in 1908 in western Thailand, only two women had been fully ordained as Buddhist nuns in the more than 700 years of Thai monastic Buddhism. Lamai married and had children, before she sought ordination. She had to go to Taiwan, where she received full ordination from Chinese nuns in 1971.

She worked tirelessly to provide a welcoming place to women who sought to live as nuns in the face of resistance from the Thai male monastic hierarchy, which did not (and still does not) recognize women's full ordination.

By the time of her passing in 2003, Bhikkhunī Voramai had established a fully fledged monastery near Bangkok. Her daughter, Chatsumarn Kabilsingh, had received full ordination as Bhikkhunī Dhammananda and was ready to take up her mother's mantle.

Dhammananda tells a story about her mother that exemplifies her focus on meditation. Venerable Voramai, just after receiving ordination, was asked by a young man whether she kept all 311 precepts of the monastic order. She replied that she kept one precept, that of watching her mind.

128 Breathe

A common meditation practice is based on mindfulness of the breath. The breath is, for obvious reasons, always with us, so it is a convenient and easily accessible support for meditation.

Find a comfortable position, preferably sitting, either in the 'lotus' or the 'semi-lotus' position, or on a chair with your feet firmly planted on the floor and your back straight (imagine being a ballet dancer, or having a thread holding your spine all the way up to the top of your head), chin slightly tucked in, shoulders opened and relaxed and hands on your lap.

Start by taking a few deep breaths and by feeling your body here and now. Notice where you feel the breath the most: Is it at the nostrils when you're breathing in and out? Is it in the belly? Or the chest? Or maybe in the shoulders as they rise gently with each in-breath?

Once you've identified that area, let your awareness rest lightly on it, observing the breath as it comes and goes. Without any doubt, your mind will wander away. When you notice that your attention has wandered, bring it back to the breath gently. When it wanders again, bring it back again. This is mindfulness.

129   A gold star

In his book *Atomic Habits*, the habit guru James Clear explains that the practice of habit tracking has such good results because it makes a behaviour obvious, attractive and satisfying. In other words, habit tracking helps us become mindful of a behaviour at every step.

Setting up habit tracking, whether the old-fashioned way on paper or digitally (beware the risk of distraction there!), establishes your intention mentally *and* visually. Marking it off with a gold star or a cross or, my favourite, a flower sticker rewards you for the accomplishment and helps you be accountable to yourself. Moreover, as parents of teenagers well know, keeping a streak going is a strong motivation – and is visual evidence of your progress.

Essentially, habit tracking helps you be mindful of the behaviours you want to adopt and keeps you on track.

130   Accept the sensations: S. N. Goenka

S. N. Goenka was not what you would expect of a meditation teacher. A successful and prominent businessman, born in Burma (Myanmar) in 1924, he described himself as 'short-tempered and egotistic'. In his thirties, seeking relief from debilitating headaches, he followed the advice of a friend and approached U Ba King, a meditation teacher. U Ba King first refused to teach him, arguing that Goenka needed a doctor instead.

Goenka later explained that it was this rejection that attracted him because it showed that U Ba King was not interested in gaining fame from teaching such an important and wealthy person. Eventually, U Ba King relented and taught Goenka the *vipassana* method, which is, in a fundamental way, the basis for all mindfulness techniques practised today.

Goenka ultimately left his business to his family and became a full-time meditation teacher. His influence is still felt not only through his numerous students, such as American meditation teachers Sharon Salzberg, Joseph Goldstein and Daniel Goleman, but also through countless meditation centres around the world.

In these centres, the ten-day silent meditation retreat follows the same rigorous schedule and approach that U Ba King taught Goenka. It focuses on developing mindfulness of the body and the mind through observing the breath, bodily sensations and thoughts.

The point, in Goenka's words, is to 'accept the sensations as they arise, no craving and no aversion, and realize they will pass'.

131   How does your body feel?

This exercise focuses on describing how you feel physically. One of the most important aspects of the concept of mindfulness is that we observe our experience as it is, without judgement of any sort. One way of doing this, explained in detail in an early Buddhist text, is to examine the body.

Describe, in as many details as you can and as neutrally as possible, the many sensations that you can identify in your body, starting with the head all the way down to your feet. Use your journal, a piece of paper or a device and be as descriptive as you can.

132   The teaching of the Buddhas

To avoid all evil, to cultivate good, and to cleanse one's mind – this is the teaching of the Buddhas.

The Buddha, *Dhammapada*, verse 183

133   Look around you

The great Buddhist teacher Thich Nhat Hanh often said that the conditions for happiness are in us and around us. What brings you joy? Is it the golden light of the morning sunshine? Is it the soft and quiet blanket of snow that greets you when you look outside? Is it your child's small hand in yours? Is it the help you gave a friend or a relative?

Look within and around you to see all that brings you joy and happiness.

134   Devices, mindfully

People around the world spend an increasing amount of time on digital devices, whether for work or entertainment. Studies have shown that the average American spends more than seven hours a day staring at a screen (compared to over three hours a day for continental Europeans). More alarmingly, American teenagers spend more than seven hours on their devices not including homework time, meaning that they spend nearly all their waking time on a device. We know that this can cause a range of issues, from social isolation to overeating.

What about you? How satisfied are you with your use of devices? Are there virtual activities that you'd like to perform IRL (in real life) more often? For example, shopping, having a chat with a friend, going to the library for newspapers and books, watching a film?

Make a list of these options and plan how you will cut down your use of digital devices and replace it with real-life activities.

135   Grab your thesaurus!

Traditional Buddhist texts tend to be very repetitive. One reason is that they were transmitted orally for many centuries and repetition, of course, helps memory.

Part of the repetitive pattern is that they use many quasi-synonyms to describe the world and human experience. For example, a happy mind is not just a happy mind, it is peaceful, imperturbable, joyful and enraptured. The profusion of adjectives helps paint a vivid and colourful world even millennia later. The use of a range of words also deepens our understanding of the texts.

Research has shown that being able to identify your emotions and those of others is a crucial component of psychological and emotional health. Expanding one's vocabulary about emotions and feelings helps us to be more precise and to differentiate between them.

Use different terms to describe your experience and expand your self-understanding.

136   Discipline the mind

Do no harm.

Practise what is good.

Discipline the mind.

The Buddha, *The Dhammapada*, verse 183

137   Eating mindfully

Make time today, at least 30 minutes, for your breakfast, lunch or dinner. Help yourself and take a moment. Acknowledge that the work of many has gone into the food you are about to eat. Be thankful to them. Be thankful that you are able to eat.

Take a first mouthful. Put down your utensil. Chew slowly. Notice the taste of the food you are chewing: Is it salty? Sweet? Sour? Bitter? Meaty? Notice its texture: Is it smooth or crunchy? Is it hard or soft? Is it tough or chewy? There is no need to judge whether you like it or not. It is enough to savour its taste and texture.

Once you have swallowed that first bite, notice the sensation as it passes through your oesophagus and reaches your stomach. Take a slow breath and pick up your utensil again for a second mouthful. As you resume chewing, notice again the taste and texture.

Take your time chewing. One of the proponents of the macrobiotic diet, Michio Kushi, used to say that we should 'drink the solids and chew the liquids' to insist that we should eat slowly.

Finish eating in the same manner, chewing each mouthful carefully, savouring the different tastes and textures. How does it feel to be eating mindfully?

138   Mindfulness for all: Khun Mae Siri Krinchai

Siri Krinchai (1917–2011) dedicated herself to making mindfulness meditation available to all. She started teaching meditation in her house in Bangkok, Thailand, and developed a simple one-week meditation workshop that was very popular with families with children.

Many people were grateful to her for making Buddhist teachings and meditation easily accessible and for the beneficial impact that it had on their lives. They called her *Khun Mae*, 'Honourable Mother', to show their respect and affection.

Khun Mae made mindfulness accessible for a wide range of people, including children. She showed that you don't have to be a special kind of person or go to a monastery or a temple to practise meditation. Khun Mae believed mindfulness can be practised by all, including the young or the busiest people.

139   Focus on your mind

In this exercise, focus on your mind and your emotions. One of the most important aspects of the practice of mindfulness is that we observe our experience as it is. One way of doing this is to examine the content of your mind.

Describe in as much detail as you can and as neutrally as possible what's happening in your mind. Contemporary Buddhist teachers advise their students to 'name' the content of their thoughts. This helps separate the perception or emotion from the sense of who we are as a person.

For example, instead of writing 'I am happy' or 'I am angry', you can write 'There is happiness' or 'There is anger'. Instead of thinking 'I hear a car outside' or 'I feel warm', think 'hearing' or 'warmth'.

140   All things

Buddha-nature is all things. All things are buddha-nature. This person,
this body, this mind, this world, this wind and this rain. This daily
routine, going, living, sitting and lying down. Sadness, joy, action
and inaction. The stick and the wand. The Buddha's smile,
the transmission of the teachings, their study and practice.
The pine tree and the bamboo tree.

Dōgen (1200–53) Dōgen, *Shōbōgenzō* IV

141　Break up with your pain

Jon Kabat-Zin, the founder of the Mindfulness-Based Stress Reduction programme, uses mindfulness practices to help alleviate chronic pain in patients whom conventional medicine can no longer help.

The basis of the programme is to become fully aware of the pain rather than trying to avoid it. The pain becomes an object of attention, just like any other. Kabat-Zin explains that the physical sensation of pain can be observed separately from the usual alarm reaction that tells us that it is painful and must be avoided.

The patient brings mindfulness to the sensation of pain and notes its location, extent and qualities. For example: Is it warm? Cold? Pulsating? Throbbing? Dull? Acute? Then the patient notes the reactions (thoughts and emotions) that accompany the pain. For example, thoughts such as 'I can't bear this', 'It's horrible', 'Why me?' or feelings of anger, depression or anxiety are observed as they arise in the mind.

The goal is to realize that the physical (or mental) sensation of pain is separate from the reaction and that the reaction is just a mental event, no more, no less than the thought 'The sky is blue today' and the reaction 'I like this weather'.

Next time you feel discomfort or pain, try separating the sensation of pain from your reaction to it.

142　To browse or not to browse

Are you about to grab your phone or open up your browser to do a search? STOP! Close your eyes for a moment. Take a deep breath. Ask yourself: 'Do I need to do this, right now?' 'Will this piece of information be useful for my day? Will it be useful to others?' Ask yourself: 'What is this urge aiming to alleviate or satisfy?'

Maybe you need a break or a distraction. Walk around the block instead. If that's not possible, take 200 steps around the room or walk to the mailbox. Or do a few stretches. Pay attention to the sensations in your feet as they touch and lift up from the ground and the sensations in your body as it moves through space. Breathe slowly and mindfully, noticing the movement and sensations of your breath in and out of your nostrils.

Now, if you still need to, go ahead and pick up your phone or open your browser.

143   Let it RAIN

Being mindful requires becoming aware of our thoughts, emotions and feelings. To help deal specifically with difficult emotions, mindfulness meditation teacher Michele McDonald developed the RAIN practice. RAIN stands for Recognize, Accept, Investigate and Nonidentify.

First, we *recognize* that thoughts, emotions and feelings are present and *accept* them just as they are without trying to ignore them or push them away. We acknowledge that thoughts, emotions and feelings arise and dissolve continually, giving them space as the sky gives space to clouds.

Then we *investigate* and explore by being curious about what is happening in our body. Where are sensations most present? What do they feel like? Ask yourself: Is this pleasant, unpleasant or neutral?

Finally, we *nonidentify* by observing what is happening in the body and mind just as that: sensations and thoughts that arise and pass and are not us. Remember to drop the judgemental mind, not even to judge itself. Judgements are like any other thought: they arise and pass.

Just observe and let it be, staying with the flow of experience as it unfolds.

144 Tea (or coffee) meditation

Do you drink your morning drink on the go? While you're preparing for work? Getting the kids ready for school? Do you even know what it tastes like? While I will only have tea in the morning, you can do this meditation with any drink – although a cocktail might defeat the purpose of being mindful.

Start by holding the cup in your hands. Feel its texture, its temperature. Is it rough or smooth? Warm or cold? Is it glass, ceramic, metal, plastic or paper? Breathe deeply as you feel the cup in your hands. Now bring the cup to your lips. Pay attention as you bring it up and tilt it slightly. Pay attention to the sensations of the cup meeting your lips, the liquid flowing into your mouth. Let it rest there for a moment. How does it feel? Breathe deeply before swallowing. When you swallow, feel the liquid travel to your stomach and become part of you. Experience the sensation of warmth or cool as it spreads in your stomach. Now take another sip and repeat.

You can do this meditation for as long as you wish: just one mindful sip will bring you into the present moment and make you feel more alive.

145 Live spiritually

According to Sulak Sivaraksa, a Thai Buddhist activist, both contemplation and social activism are necessary to effect change for the better. For him, they illuminate, inform and support each other. Born in Thailand in 1933, Sulak Sivaraksa has been engaged in both for his whole life. In the 1960s he worked with Buddhist monks in Thailand to sensitize them to social and environmental issues.

Ajahn (teacher) Sulak believes Buddhism should focus on the teachings of the Buddha, such as mindfulness, non-violence and interconnectedness, to achieve social change locally and globally. He also supports inter-religious dialogue and established a group focusing on religion and society that includes a wide range of people from diverse traditions.

In 1995 he received the Right Livelihood Award for his 'vision, activism and spiritual commitment in the quest for a development process that is rooted in democracy, justice and cultural integrity', and in 1998 he received the UNPO Human Rights Award.

Sulak embodies his belief that 'people seeking to live spiritually must be concerned with their social and physical environment'.

146   Blue like an orange

Where are you right now? Grab your journal or a piece of paper. Look around you and describe your environment. Are you sitting at a desk or a table? Or maybe even in a recliner or on a sofa (my favourite place to journal).

Observe your environment. What colours are the walls? Or, if you are outside, what trees or plants can you see? Be as precise as you can be. How many chairs are there in the room? How many trees in your field of vision? What colour is the sky? Is it cloudy or clear? Give as many details as you can. For example, write: 'The furniture in this room is angular and dark. It's dusty. Or it looks well cared for.'

Use metaphors if you wish. French poet Paul Éluard once wrote, 'The earth is blue like an orange', a metaphor that brings together images of celestial happiness associated with the colour blue and earthly happiness associated with a juicy and fragrant fruit.

What does your environment evoke for you?

147   Swept away

Mindfulness of the body, speech and mind is a shelter,
a harbour, an island, a refuge and a support in this world
swept away by old age, illness and death.

The Buddha, *Anguttara Nikāya*, 3.51

148   Embrace your sadness

In her book *How to Be Sad*, journalist Helen Russell claims that she learned how to be happier by embracing her sadness. She explains that, in contemporary European cultures, sadness is considered an unacceptable emotion that should always be avoided.

We shun our sadness, hide it and pretend we're okay. We also don't know (because we haven't learned) how to deal with other people's sadness, sometimes even ignoring sad events for fear of saying or doing the wrong thing.

Helen Russell encourages us to embrace our sadness. She says that it has something to tell us. Sadness is a natural emotion that arises when something goes wrong. Whether it is a life-changing event like the death of someone dear to us or a minor setback, sadness is a signal that needs to be acknowledged and listened to.

By being mindful of your sadness, you'll be sad better and you'll be happier.

149   A shower meditation

Start a new meditation practice. You're probably thinking that you have too many things to do in a single day to add another item to your to-do list. In this case, improvise a habit-bundling meditation.

Do you shower every day? Try a shower meditation. Burn a stick of incense or turn off the light and put on a candle – maybe just dim the light. As you undress, visualize yourself taking off the burdens of the day. This is your space, your time – use a timer if you have time constraints.

This is an opportunity to be fully present with yourself and to this shower. Take three breaths. Be aware of your body as you breathe deeply. Turn on the water and step into the shower. Feel the texture of the floor under your feet, the warm air around you, the water running over you. Simply experience these sensations, without judgement.

You might think thoughts related to your appearance, or work, or relationships. Acknowledge each thought and refocus on your senses: What are you touching, smelling, seeing and hearing right now?

Be present with every movement and action – soaping yourself, washing your hair, rinsing. Are there pleasant, unpleasant or neutral sensations and feelings? Just feel them and acknowledge their qualities. They are not good or bad; they are your experience in this moment. When you have finished your shower, give thanks for this moment of meditation. Make it a morning or evening practice.

150   No phone today

Just joking! Or not. It's up to you. Can you spend a day without using your mobile phone? I challenge you to try it. Plan the day before so that you can prepare and think carefully about how you will do it.

You can use your landline (if you still have one) to call your friends. You can write a real letter on a physical piece of paper (have you ever written one?). You can go to the cinema and watch a film on a big screen. You can go for a walk alone or with a friend – in which case you might want to arrange this ahead of time, without forgetting to tell your friend that you'll be offline. You can read a book, or a newspaper made of paper and printed with ink.

As you go through your phoneless day, observe the urge that will no doubt arise to pick up your phone, to check 'very quickly' one thing or another. Observe how your mind will tell you that you *need* to look at your phone just for a moment, that *this* is really important. Notice the urge, take a deep breath and release it.

How did your day go? What did you learn about yourself?

CHAPTER 6

ETHICS

151   The Five Precepts

The basic Buddhist ethical framework is based on the Five Precepts. These precepts are not expressed as prohibitions. Instead, they advise to refrain from harming living beings, from speaking untruthfully or with malice, from taking things that are not given, from sexual misconduct, and from consuming substances that impair our mind and judgement.

The wording of the precepts shows an understanding that, more often than not, we will engage in these behaviours but that we can still aspire to refrain from them. Similarly, the way the behaviours are described is broad enough that it gives us the possibility of being as loose or as strict as we want or, most likely, can be.

Accepting that we will sometimes fail acknowledges our basic humanity. By gently accepting our weaknesses, we make space for progress.

152   What is good?

How do you know good from bad? Right from wrong? You have doubtless acquired some moral standards, consciously and unconsciously, from your upbringing and culture, but have you made a deliberate and honest effort to discern your *own* values?

Emotional reactions are a good way to determine whether our actions agree with our personal values. A twinge of regret or subtle unease alert us to a discrepancy between what we believe and what we do. In contrast, the warmth of satisfaction or the rush of joy pervade us when we act in harmony with our principles.

Write about a time when you felt that an action matched your values. What was the action? How did it feel while you were performing it? How did it feel afterwards? How does it feel now that you are remembering it?

153   Visākhā's sense of decorum

When Visākhā was a young child of seven years, she went with her grandfather to listen to the Buddha who was visiting the town of Baddhiya and giving teachings in King Bimbisara's park. It is said that when she heard the Buddha that day, she attained a great spiritual realization.

Visākhā Migaramātā is renowned in the Pāli canon of Theravāda Buddhism as the most generous laywoman supporter of the Buddha and his community. Indeed, there are many accounts of her generosity and lifelong commitment to the Buddha and of her support to the monks and nuns.

She was very concerned, in particular, that they should comport themselves in ways that would elicit esteem and reverence from the local population who, for the most part, were not followers of the Buddha.

One day, she saw nuns from the nearby monastery bathing in the river. She then suggested that they use bathing cloths, so that they would not be naked in public. People in ancient India did not feel respectful towards anyone who did not behave in socially sanctioned ways, such as not appearing naked publicly.

Visākhā had a keen sense of propriety and decorum and a deep understanding that society often requires external evidence of moral standards, a concern that challenges us to reflect on our own sense of morality.

How do you differentiate between your own sense of right and wrong and social mores?

154   The path of freedom and joy

The wording of the Buddhist ethical precepts emphasizes abstention and restraint rather than prohibition. This emphasis acknowledges a deep truth about human beings: we *will* fail to uphold our values. We will try again and again, and we will fail again and again.

Cultivating mindfulness does not mean that you will not fail. Being more mindful, though, means that you will catch yourself failing sooner and thus will get back on track faster. Allied with self-compassion, mindfulness practice helps us accept with gentle awareness the imperfections that make us human.

Only when we embrace our imperfections without judgement can we unlock the path of freedom and joy.

155   Refrain from harm

The first Buddhist precept is to refrain from harming any living being. Note that the word used is not 'killing' but 'harming'. Evidently, not harming is much broader than not killing. Not harming living beings extends from not killing anyone to renouncing any harmful activity.

In Jainism, a religious tradition that developed at the same time as Buddhism, this is the concept of *ahiṃsā* (non-injury), which culminates in abjuring any action that might cause harm to another being. For example, Jain monks typically cover their mouths with a cloth to avoid inhaling small creatures as they breathe, and they sweep the ground before them to prevent crushing insects as they walk.

In Buddhism, vegetarianism is valued and commonly practised, especially in East Asia. In North America and Europe, many Buddhists are even vegan. Others opt out of financial organizations that invest in armaments or in prisons. Others yet take a more active stance and work or volunteer for peace organizations, or for non-human animal welfare and other such organizations.

What other ways do you think it is possible to refrain from harming living beings?

156   Tormented by remorse

When one does not do commendable and wholesome things, and does not protect those who live in fear and, instead, does evil, ruthless and cruel things, one is tormented by remorse.

When one does commendable and wholesome things, and protects those who live in fear and avoid doing evil, ruthless and cruel things, that one lives without torment.

The Buddha, *Itivuttaka*, 30–31

157   Not feeling like it?

Have you ever noticed that we don't always act in the way we aspire to? For example, I want to exercise regularly, read books and paint watercolours, yet when I finally have some time to myself, I end up on the sofa scrolling through social media.

The mind and the body naturally reach for easiness and effortlessness. The trick is to ignore this inclination and instead simply do what you aspire to. Don't wait to feel like it. Most days you won't. Even if it's just for a few minutes, do it. Not only will you be happier for it but, most importantly, you will be living the life you want to live.

And, of course, sometimes that means spending the afternoon on the sofa!

158   Refrain from taking what is not given

I thought I knew what generosity is, but the second Buddhist precept forced me to think more deeply. This precept enjoins us to 'not take what is not given'. At first sight, this phrase seems like an awkward translation of an ancient Indian Pāli expression, but it compels us to reflect on what constitutes theft and associated behaviours. 'Taking what is not given' goes beyond not stealing and requires us to be more mindful about everything we use.

For example, think about our impact on the Earth, and on future generations: do we take more than our fair share? Earth Overshoot Day marks the day in the year when humanity's consumption exceeds what the Earth can regenerate during that year – in other words, what we take from future generations. This day arrives earlier and earlier every year – the first time it was calculated, in 1987, it occurred in late October; in 2021 it was 29 July. It's like eating all the food you need for the week by Wednesday so that you need to borrow next week's food. This can't last very long.

Reflecting on our consumption and becoming more mindful of what our real needs are (as opposed to what advertisements tell us) is one way of 'not taking what is not given'. Think of one or two things you can give up because they are not given. Resolve to give them up.

159   What is your yardstick?

The two foremost Buddhist virtues are wisdom and compassion. They are the yardstick by which action is measured.

What are your two most important values? If you don't have a clear idea, think about what is important to you. For example, would you rather support an organization that educates children or one that advocates for criminal justice reform? Or for environmental protection? Or one that supports the arts? Where are you most likely to spend money outside of your basic needs?

Remember, there are no wrong or right values – values are choices we make about what is meaningful to us.

With this exercise you can better understand how your actions align with your values and identify how you can uphold them more consistently. Ultimately, values are what your life is really about.

160   Mingyur Rinpoche escapes from his monastery

One night in June 2011, like the Buddha when he left the royal palace, Yongey Mingyur Rinpoche left his monastery in Bodh Gaya and went on a peripatetic retreat. He told no one of his plan to become a wandering ascetic, leaving behind the comfortable and busy life of a monastic abbot and internationally known meditation master. For four years, he slept on the streets of India's holy cities and meditated in the caves of the Himalayas.

Born in 1975 in Nepal, into a renowned Tibetan Buddhist family (his father was a well-known meditation teacher and his mother a descendant of two Tibetan kings), Yongey Mingyur Rinpoche had already spent a lot of his life learning the highest Buddhist teachings from some of the greatest Tibetan masters, but he felt that his life at the monastery did not support his pursuit of the highest realization.

Early in his travels, when he was living on the streets of Kushinagar, the town where the Buddha died, Mingyur Rinpoche says he suffered an episode of food poisoning that nearly killed him. This experience profoundly transformed him and left him feeling free 'like a bird soaring in the sky'.

Since returning to his monastery, Mingyur Rinpoche has changed his emphasis from formal teachings and meditation to a focus on daily life and the role meditation can play in changing our everyday ordinary life.

What role does it play in yours?

161   Push-ups for the mind

Mindfulness and ethical conduct are intimately related in Buddhism. Ultimately, the purpose of developing mindfulness is to live a fully ethical life and, according to Buddhist principles, an ethical life is a happy life.

When we calm the mind and are aware of our thoughts, emotions and urges, we are more apt to act according to our values and therefore to be more content and serene.

As with all things, preparedness is necessary. In the same way that we don't set out on a full marathon without training first, we need to train the mind to be still and aware. Neuroscientist Amishi Jha's research indicates that 12 minutes of mindfulness meditation a day provides a good basis for living a more mindful life.

Think of it as your push-up training for the mind!

162   Refrain from sexual misconduct

Like many religious traditions, Buddhism tends to be conservative when it comes to sexual mores. In the more socially liberal environment of the modern world, the third Buddhist precept of 'refraining from sexual misconduct' sometimes causes perplexity and even controversy.

Contemporary Buddhists endeavour to refine their understanding of what constitutes sexual misconduct in the modern world in which many more behaviours are accepted than in the past. Although there is much disagreement, one emerging consensus is that, like with the other precepts, the point is not to harm anyone, yourself or others, within sexual relationships.

When you keep in mind the first and second precepts (non-harming and not taking what is not given) in the context of the third (refraining from sexual misconduct), it is easier to decide for yourself what constitutes ethical sexual conduct.

163   Watch your thoughts

The wise one should watch their thoughts, which are difficult to see. Watching one's thoughts, one attains happiness. When thoughts are untroubled, when thoughts are calm, one attains happiness.

The Buddha, *Dhammapada*, 33–9

164   Give yourself a good past (and a happy present)

The old saying warns that we cannot change our past.

True. But we can create a better one by acting now.

Buddhist emphasis on moral conduct is not born out of an antiquated sense of morality. Instead, it is founded on a clear understanding of human psychology. We cannot be truly happy and content when we fail to live up to our personal moral standards. We face regret and even guilt when we act in what we deem to be morally reprehensible ways.

When you ground your actions in mindful ethics, you bequeath yourself a good past and live a happy present.

165   One virtue a day

It is said that Benjamin Franklin (1706–1790), the American inventor and statesman, had a list of 13 virtues that he wanted to cultivate. He devoted time to each virtue separately and kept a little notebook in which he wrote whether he had succeeded in that particular virtue each day. When he felt that he had sufficiently mastered a virtue, he moved on to the next one on his list.

In a similar way, some Buddhist teachers recommend that you set an intention as you start your day and reflect on it before going to bed.

I challenge you to follow these examples of self-improvement and reflection. Cultivate your chosen virtues one at a time, making sure to dedicate some time each day to examine your progress.

166   Refrain from wrong speech

Do you sometimes find yourself in a 'sit-and-bitch' session only to regret later some of the things you said? The fourth Buddhist precept enjoins us to refrain from wrong speech. Wrong speech, defined broadly, includes anything that has the potential to be harmful, and gossiping is without any doubt potentially harmful.

Having a broad category such as wrong speech encourages us to consider what *for us* is wrong speech. You must actively decide whether a joke or a piece of gossip is acceptable (or not) to you. The hesitation or discomfort we sometimes experience as we speak is a warning from our moral sense. It is telling us that the joke about someone's look, or the comment about a friend's behaviour, is 'wrong speech'.

Ask yourself this question before speaking, writing or posting on social media: 'Would I say this to this person if they were sitting in front of me right now?' If the answer is negative, don't speak, write or post.

What are your criteria for deciding whether you should say something or not?

167   How do you refrain from harm?

In this writing exercise, reflect on what doing no harm means for you. What does it mean not to do harm to yourself? In other words, what physical and mental actions and behaviours do you seek to refrain from in order not to harm yourself? What does it mean not to harm your loved ones? What about people around you? What does it mean not to harm the larger community? The non-human world?

For each of these areas, consider what you are already doing not to do harm, but also what else you could do. Simple and small actions make the fabric of our lives, so think about the small habits you have or can develop, such as giving up unhealthy foods, avoiding single-use plastics, or not speaking in anger.

168 No justice without love: Reverend angel Kyodo williams

Reverend angel Kyodo williams believes that, without justice, there cannot be love, and that, without love, there cannot be justice. To achieve justice, she says, inner change is as necessary as outer and collective change, since our minds are not independent of collective history and experience.

Born in 1969 in New York City, Reverend angel Kyodo williams is an ordained Zen priest and is the second Black woman recognized as a teacher in Zen Buddhism. She is the founder of the Center for Transformative Change. Her books and articles have explored the personal and collective experience of being Black in American Buddhism, and she has been actively raising political and social awareness in North American Buddhist circles.

Her book *Radical Dharma* warns that there cannot be collective awakening in a context of racial injustice. For Reverend angel, the Buddhist community must expand its boundaries to include all beings, just as the Buddha accepted all regardless of caste, class, rank, gender and race.

169 Where does harming begin and end?

Buddhist basic ethical precepts enjoin us to avoid unwholesome actions. They tell us to refrain from harming, from taking what is not given, from harmful speech, from sexual misconduct and from intoxicants.

The wide scope of these precepts compels us to consider what they mean *for us*. Does harming stop at killing (a common understanding of the precept) or does it go further for you? What about taking what is not given? In the same way that Buddhist societies must engage with their understanding of the precepts, individuals must engage with ethics as a continuing life project.

You can embrace this practice and contemplate what these principles, or other principles you hold, mean in your life and how you choose to embody them.

170   Moral self-examination

The Buddhist monastic community is regulated by a set of norms, rules and practices that provide a framework for behaviour and moral self-examination. The daily routine, the recitation of the monastic code, the rituals and other communal activities articulate and support this ethical framework.

Like monks and nuns, our life is regulated by a set of norms, rules and practices that shape our attitudes and behaviours in ways we are often unaware of. Most of us, especially if we don't belong to a religious community, lack a formal structure within which to conduct moral self-examination.

Give yourself time to identify your norms and values, and to examine your conduct in light of these norms and values. It will help you live with integrity and honesty.

171   If a person does good

If a person does good, let them do it again and again. Let them aspire to it, as doing good leads to happiness.

The Buddha, *Dhammapada*, 118

172 No gossip

Who doesn't love a piece of juicy gossip? It is hard to resist, isn't it? The Buddhist precept of refraining from harmful speech includes refraining from gossip because gossip not only can harm those it targets, but also harms those who engage in it. They see another human being as an object of ridicule and derision and fail to acknowledge their common humanity.

Another reason not to gossip is that sociological and psychological studies have found it negatively affects social cohesion, trust and self-perception.

When caught up in a situation where gossip is shared, ask yourself what would happen if the person targeted could hear you. No doubt the answer will tell you whether to stay quiet or carry on.

173 What do your emotions say about your behaviour?

Buddhist monks and nuns follow a set of rules that lay out unacceptable or problematic actions and behaviours (227 rules for monks and 311 for nuns in the Theravāda tradition). The most egregious actions are those that entail 'defeat'. Effectively, by committing the action, a monk is no longer a monk, a nun is no longer a nun.

What these 'defeat' rules have in common is that first they automatically cause the monk or nun who violates them to 'fall away' from the monastic life. There is no need for 'excommunication' or punishment – one is no longer a monk or a nun. As the scholar Maria Heim explains, these actions cause great remorse, an emotion so strong and pervasive that it inevitably prevents the offenders from pursuing the monastic and spiritual life. They are no longer in communion with the monastic community.

Emotions illuminate our moral behaviour. How and when do your emotions alert you about your behaviour?

174   Use Right Speech

Think of an issue you have strong opinions about and on which you disagree with someone either in your close entourage or in the wider world. What is the issue? What do you believe?

Write to the person you disagree with using Right Speech. Use positive descriptions and kind words. Explain how you feel about the issue. Imagine why they hold their position: remember to use caring and empathetic statements. Assume they are seeking goodness in themselves and in the world by holding this position, just as you are by holding yours.

Finally, write about what you have learned from doing this exercise.

175   Remembering ethical principles: Māghā Pūjā Day

Māghā Pūjā Day is a festival in Theravāda Buddhist countries that commemorates the Buddha establishing the rules of conduct for the monastic community.

According to the tradition, some time after reaching awakening, the Buddha gathered with his followers on the full moon of the third lunar month and recited the *Ovādapātimokkha*, a short summary of Buddhist principles. It focuses on avoiding harmful actions and performing wholesome ones, as well as patience and forbearance, presenting in a nutshell the fundamental principles of Buddhist ethics.

During the Māghā Pūjā Day, Buddhists attend the temple and make offerings. Some also take this opportunity to fully uphold the Five Precepts as well as meditate and chant Buddhist texts as a way of contemplating the Buddhist ethical principles.

When do you take time to consider your ethical principles?

176   So joyful

The world is so light
It's no longer here
And so joyful
It lacks nothing.

Paul Éluard (1895–1952) 'Les petits justes', *Capitale de la douleur*

177   Even spiders and cockroaches

A Tibetan Buddhist practice of non-harming consists in avoiding killing insects or pests whenever possible. Often, Tibetan Buddhist practitioners capture spiders, mice or cockroaches they find inside and take them outside rather than use pesticides or other lethal means of getting rid of them.

Other ways of avoiding harm to other beings and the environment include being mindful of our consumption and aiming to decrease it. For example, limiting the amount of new clothing you purchase in a given season, or refraining from throwing away food.

In what other ways can you cultivate non-harming?

178   Would you give up tea or coffee?

Before it was widely adopted as an integral part of monastic life, Buddhist monks in China disagreed on whether drinking tea was an infringement of the fifth precept of avoiding mind-altering substances.

Some argued that since tea is energizing (because of its caffeine content, as we now know), it was helpful for staying awake during meditation. Others countered that, because it affects the mind, tea should be avoided. Those who favoured tea won the day, and thus started the spread of what became the most beloved drink in China.

Nowadays, similar discussions are still taking place, although not necessarily about tea. I heard the problem with mind-altering substances explained in a succinct way at a meditation retreat in France. It is not so much the substances themselves but the fact that, under their influence, we are much more likely to break every other precept.

I'm still not willing to give up my morning tea, but I understand better why many religions either prohibit or restrict the use of intoxicants. What do you think about it?

179 The doors of heaven

Hakuin Ekaku (1689–1769) was a Zen master well known for his unexpected and startling responses. One time, it is said, a samurai visited him and asked him if paradise and hell really existed.

Hakuin scoffed, 'What kind of a soldier are you? You look like a beggar!' The soldier, indignant, jumped to his feet and put his hand on his sword.

Hakuin, amused, continued to rile him. 'What kind of sword is that? You couldn't cut my head off with this blunt edge!' Enraged, the soldier drew the sword out of its sheath. Hakuin warned him, 'This is how you open the doors of hell.'

The samurai immediately understood the master's wisdom and restraint and sheathed his sword, bowing deeply. 'And this is how you open the doors of heaven,' Hakuin said.

How will you open the doors of heaven?

180 Act on your values

Our values are crucial to our sense of identity, although we are not always entirely conscious or intentional about them. Being more mindful and deliberate about our life values deepens the meaning of our life beyond the day-to-day routine.

Make a resolution to bring mindfulness to your ethical values. Every day, reflect on your values as you wake up and choose one or two ways in which you will implement one or two of your values. At the end of the day, reflect on what you did, how it made you feel and what, if anything, you would do differently.

Pat yourself on the back and repeat!

CHAPTER 7

GENEROSITY

181   Develop generosity

Generosity is a fundamental virtue in many religious traditions. In Buddhist texts, generosity is described as arising from two positive motivations: non-attachment and friendliness. Indeed, to give something away, we need to develop non-attachment to that thing and to feel warmly towards the person we give it to.

Buddhists around the world show their generosity by making offerings to the Buddha, Dharma and Sangha. The most common offerings are the four 'requisites' of lodgings, monastic robes, food and medicine. By making these regular offerings, Buddhists show and embody their support to the monastic community as an institution and as the transmitters and preservers of the Buddha's teachings. By making offerings, they also cultivate the virtue of generosity.

In your own life, what do you support or wish to support in a regular way? How do you cultivate and develop the virtue of generosity?

182   Giving what's dearest: the story of Vessantara

It is said that in one of his past lives, the Buddha was a prince named Vessantara who gave everything away: his kingdom, his wife and his children. His story is still one of the best known in South-East Asia – it's staged in plays, performed on TV and pictured in comic books.

Today, the idea of giving away your children or spouse as if they were your property seems bizarre, but in the ancient Indian context the story of Vessantara illustrated the pinnacle of generosity: the prince, by giving away what was dearest to him, perfected this virtue.

In fact, Vessantara's story is the penultimate act, or even a rehearsal, for the Buddha's last grand act of generosity when, in order to pursue the ascetic path for the welfare of all beings, he gives up his kingdom, his wife, Yasodhara, and his newborn baby, Rahula, and becomes a renouncer.

These two stories evoke detachment and generosity at the highest level. Vessantara gave what was dearest to him to others whom, he felt, needed them more than he did. The Buddha gave up his kingdom and family to seek liberation from suffering and to share his knowledge and wisdom to benefit all.

Naturally, we cannot all be like the Buddha and his earlier incarnation, Vessantara, but these stories may inspire us to be more generous towards others and less attached to our own needs and desires.

Think about people in your life who inspire you to be more generous. In what ways do you follow in their footsteps?

183   The rewards of giving

If beings knew, as I know, the rewards of giving and sharing, they would not eat without sharing, nor would they let selfishness grip their mind. Even if it were their last piece, their last mouthful, they will not eat without sharing it, if someone is there to share it with.

The Buddha, *Itivuttaka*, 1.26

184   What is generosity for you?

In Buddhism, to be truly generous, an action must be wholehearted and without regrets.

Take your journal or a piece of paper and write down an instance in which you were truly generous, whether you gave your time, your attention, material goods or money. Describe what your generous action consisted of: What did you give and to whom? How did it feel during and after the gift? How did the person or persons feel?

List ways in which you can repeat this action so that it becomes a practice.

185   Act on your generosity

As you probably have experienced, it is not always easy to be generous. Often, we think of giving something – a gift, food or clothing, money, assistance to someone, or to an organization we want to support – but… life is busy and we put it off until later. Except later never comes because life keeps being busy.

Resolve to act on your generous thoughts more often. If the present moment is not convenient, make a note so that you won't forget and, as soon as you can, carry out that generous thought: drop off food at the local food bank, call that friend or relative, sign up for the soup kitchen, send that money, or smile at those you meet during the day.

Whatever it is, don't waste your generous thoughts.

186   What first step will you take?

The basic Buddhist virtue of generosity is often described as the first step on the spiritual path. When you are generous, you turn the focus away from yourself to take into consideration other beings, their needs and desires. In other words, you bring others into what constitutes *your self*. By sharing what you have with others, you make them part of you and your sense of self expands.

Think about the first three steps you can take on this path. What practice of generosity will you undertake?

187   Stack of cards

When was the last time you received a real letter or card? Although I appreciate the wonders of technology that help us connect more easily and rapidly with loved ones around the world, I believe receiving a piece of handwritten mail is a delightful surprise.

And so, thinking that others may enjoy it too, I keep a box of pretty cards, envelopes and stamps at home to make it easier for me to send birthday cards, thank-you notes or even a random note to a friend. When the occasion arises, I just need to pull out the box, choose an appropriate card, write it, stamp it and stop at the postbox on my way to work.

What habit can you develop to keep you connected to those you care about in a way meaningful to you?

188   What can you give?

Generosity is often thought of as giving material goods or money. However, Buddhist texts explain that there are actually three types of things that we can give away.

The first thing we can give is our attention: turning away from oneself, we can focus our attention on others. Whether they are other people, issues or causes, we can make a conscious effort to focus on supporting their goals and needs.

The second thing we can give, of course, is material goods and money.

Finally, we can give our time to those around us, or to a cause, for example spending time with relatives or friends, or volunteering for an organization whose work we support.

What can you give? Whom can you give to? To get you started, identify one or two people to whom you will give your attention, fully and without distraction.

189   Juzhi cannot answer

Legend says that when Juzhi (677–744) was a young monk who had been studying the Buddhist sutras for many years, he was visited by a nun. She circled him three times, as was the custom, and challenged him to say something. Juzhi was dumbstruck and could not utter a single word.

As the nun made to leave, Juzhi stammered, 'It's late, why don't you stay the night?' The nun glared at him and replied, 'Say something and I will stay.' Again, Juzhi was left speechless, and the nun left. Juzhi, feeling miserable, decided that he must leave the monastery to seek a true master.

The next day, the renowned master Hangzhou Tianlong arrived at the monastery.

When have you been left speechless only to find that life gave you what you needed?

190   Make a 'generosity list'

Buddhists usually give four things to monks and nuns: food, robes, lodging and medicine. Having a clear and straightforward idea of how they can be generous on a regular basis makes it easier to develop the virtue of generosity.

Take your journal or a piece of paper and write down your generosity list. Think about the three major 'things' you can give: your attention, money (or material goods) and your time. What can you give on a regular basis and to whom? Be practical and honest: clearly assess the likelihood that you will be able to give these things regularly so that it becomes a practice. It does not have to be huge: a smile, a call, a cup of coffee or tea, homemade cookies – these are small things you can give daily.

To plan your practice of generosity, describe what, when and to whom you will give. How does it make you feel to be intentionally generous?

191   Joyful generosity

Have you ever seen a young child make a gift? They're often more excited about making a gift than receiving one. They choose it with attention, thinking about what will please you. Then, they can barely contain their impatience while you open the wrapping, and they look at you to see your reaction.

For children, giving is a joyful action. The Buddha felt exactly the same. When asked about the right ways of giving, he said that when giving, we should feel joyful before, during and after making the gift.

Be like a child. Practise joyful generosity!

192   Listen carefully

Your attention is a gift that does not cost much, but it is rewarding both to you and to the person you give attention to.

Next time you speak with someone, practise giving them your full and complete attention. Put away your digital devices so that they are out of your sight and cannot distract you. Focus your gaze on the person – don't stare at them but keep a soft gaze around their face. Truly listen to what they are saying, without judging or anticipating what they may be trying to say. Avoid mentally rehearsing your reply, just focus on what they are saying. Ask them open questions if you feel it is appropriate, such as 'How does this make you feel?'

Practise your generosity by being a good listener.

193   Attention

Attention is the rarest and purest form of generosity.
Simone Weil (1909–1943), *First and Last Notebooks*

194   Develop your listening skills

Giving your attention to someone is one of the most generous gifts you can make. Step it up!

For example, read a book or take a course on listening skills (yes, they do exist!) to learn to be a more attentive and mindful listener.

You will develop deeper relationships and practise an important aspect of generosity.

195 A handful of broken rice

One day, the Buddha was visiting a small town and received alms from the local inhabitants. One of the prominent dignitaries invited the Buddha and his monks to a meal in his splendid mansion. There, they were treated to a vast array of rare delicacies in a magnificent environment.

As they left the mansion, a poor old woman, who had heard that the Buddha was visiting the town, was waiting by the road. She knew it was her last opportunity to see the great teacher due to her old age and she had gathered all she had to make him an offering: a meagre handful of broken rice with which she had prepared a rice cake.

When the Buddha saw the old woman, he stopped and accepted her gift in the same way he had accepted the lavish meal from the high dignitary. As he left, he told the monks, 'You see, monks, the fruit of this old woman's generosity is much greater than the fruit of this rich merchant's generosity, because she gave all she had with all her heart.'

Think about a time when you have received a meaningful gift because of the sincerity and generosity of the giver. How did it make you feel?

196 Just like you

Develop the habit of looking people in the eyes. Not only your loved ones or your co-workers, but the barista when you pick up your coffee, the person standing next to you in a queue, or the train manager on your commute.

Look them in the eyes, greet them if appropriate, smile if it feels right. Recognize their common humanity. Just like you, they want to be happy.

Think about the people you come across and resolve to give them the gift of your attention each and every day.

197 Overcome selfishness

> With gentleness, overcome anger. With generosity,
> overcome selfishness. With truth, overcome delusion.
> The Buddha, The *Dhammapada*, verse 223

198 A gift to you

Think of a time when someone made you a gift that felt particularly generous – it need not be an expensive or extravagant gift, but anything that made you feel grateful and appreciated. For example, it could be when someone cared for you when you were ill, or inquired after you following a sad episode in your life. Or it could be something as simple as when someone took you out for a meal just because... or gave you a heartfelt compliment.

Describe what this gift was. Who gave it to you? What sort of gift was it? How did it make you feel? Be specific in your description: include as many details as you can about the context (the place, the time and the circumstances), the emotions you felt and the thoughts you had.

What conclusions can you draw from this about what generosity is for you? How can you apply it to your life?

199 Kathina: a giving festival

The festival of Kathina in Theravāda Buddhism – practised predominantly in Sri Lanka, Thailand, Cambodia, Laos and Myanmar – is celebrated at the end of the annual three-month rain retreat. During this festival, lay people make offerings of new robes to the monastic community, following a tradition established at the time of the Buddha.

It is said that monks who had travelled to stay with the Buddha for the rain retreat did not arrive in time, so they had to spend the retreat away. When the retreat ended and they were able to reach the Buddha's monastery, their robes were old and torn. The Buddha, seeing this, gave them the cloth he had received from a lay woman, demonstrating how an act of generosity grows and multiplies.

Today, it has become a favourite opportunity for lay Buddhists to practise generosity (and earn spiritual merit).

What regular opportunities do you have in your life to cultivate generosity – think about events such as birthdays, religious festivals and public holidays? Find ways in which you can make them more mindful and meaningful.

200   Mindful gifts

One of my friends is the most thoughtful person I know. His secret is that he is very attentive to what people like and enjoy. Someone mentions their passion for dark chocolate, the next time we're on an outing and we come across an artisan chocolatier, he'll pick up a box of hand-made dark chocolate. Mention a book you'd like to read and you can be sure that, on your birthday, you will receive it as a present. Or talk about your favourite Netflix show and if he comes across an article that mentions it, he will share it with you.

I truly admire his ability not only to pay attention but also to act on his generous thoughts time and time again. I have tried to emulate it – not very successfully, I must confess.

If, like me, you are a bit forgetful, make a practice of keeping track of birthdays in your calendar, and a running list of the likes and wishes of those close to you, so that you can easily act on them. Your gifts will be more thoughtful and meaningful.

201   Be generous (it's good for you!)

Generosity – giving time, money or help to others – has been shown by psychology researchers to have a positive impact not only on the recipients but also on the giver.

People who give to others tend to be happier than those who don't. They tend to live healthier and longer lives. Because being generous opens us up to others, it helps us create more meaningful relationships.

A study by Michael Norton, a Harvard researcher, showed that people engaging in concrete acts of kindness felt happier than those who had more abstract goals. Other studies have shown that acts of kindness are associated with higher levels of positive emotions, such as improved mood and higher self-esteem, and lower levels of negative emotions like stress and anxiety.

Go on, be selfish! Do something for someone!

202   Giving safety

The story of Thangthong Gyalpo (1385–1464), well known for having built bridges throughout Tibet, helps us extend our conception of generosity. Thangthong Gyalpo was a Tibetan master whose activities are a great example of giving what the Buddhists call 'freedom from fear'.

The bridges he built helped travellers cross dangerous mountain passes and rivers, increasing their safety and the likelihood that they would arrive in good time. He is said to have built 58 iron bridges, 60 wooden bridges and 118 ferries. In addition, he gave teachings on long life that are still passed on today in Tibetan Buddhism.

When we make life easier and safer for others, like Thangthong Gyalpo did in Tibet, we make the gift of safety and improve the lives of many. Think about the ways in which your contributions facilitate lives around you, whether at home, at work or even through your taxes.

Reflect and be more aware of the role we all play in our community. Enjoy the feeling of connectedness.

203   Be a mindful consumer

Being a mindful consumer is a form of generosity. By bringing your attention to what you consume and how much you consume, you live a more mindful life. Develop a practice of buying and consuming less, reusing more, and mending and repairing as much as possible.

To start, here are some ideas you can include in your mindful consumption practice. Avoid or ban one-use-only items. For example, replace sponges with washable knitted dishcloths and cotton balls with washable pads. Don't throw food away and use leftovers in creative ways. Eat less or no meat and animal products. Shop locally. Share with your friends. Change your light bulbs to energy-saving ones. Insulate your home. Avoid using motor vehicles for short distances. Use public transport for longer trips if possible, or carpool. Read about climate change. Start a climate book club. Push for corporations to be responsible. Hold your elected officials responsible for climate action.

You already know this stuff. It's time to pick two or three concrete things you have put off until now and act on them.

204   Chanting in unison

Chanting is a practice found in most Buddhist traditions. Initially, before they were written down, communal chanting was the sole way of memorizing and transmitting the teachings. The practice persisted and is found in all schools of Buddhism. In some traditions, such as the Pure Land in East Asia, it is even the most important practice.

Chanting is an embodied way to learn and commit to the teachings. It can be an important aspect of rituals, a meditative practice, and, of course, it supports learning about the Buddhist teachings.

As a communal, rhythmic and embodied activity, chanting also strengthens the feeling of connection we feel with each other and reaffirms our sense of belonging as we chant, move and breathe in unison with others.

When have you felt this sense of belonging to a community? Where can you cultivate and strengthen it?

205   Choose well!

Develop the practice of choosing the recipients of your charitable donations well.

Think about the issues that are important to you. Discuss them with your family and friends to decide which you want to support. Then, examine the organizations related to these issues and see whether their ethos agrees with your values and their actions match their words. Pay attention to where they are spending their money – for example, are they spending a lot on adverts and mailings or on the actual programmes and people they claim to help?

Once you've identified an organization you would like to support, set up a direct debit so that you don't forget or, conversely, put a reminder in your calendar.

Remember, it doesn't have to be a large amount to be helpful and for you to develop a generosity practice.

206   The greatest gift of all

According to the Buddha, the greatest gift of all is the gift of the Dharma, the Buddhist teachings. Why is teaching about the principles and virtues of Buddhism considered the greatest gift of all? Simply because, in Buddhist thought, it allows you to develop the qualities of a happier and more fulfilled life.

In a more secular environment, this gift can be expanded to include any knowledge, practice or habit that promotes your mindfulness and happiness.

Similarly, when you give good advice to someone, advice that has a positive impact on that person's life, you are giving a great gift.

207   The perfect gift

I don't know about you, but I'm always worried about not giving the appropriate gift. What if my friend doesn't like it? What if it's not good enough? Or it makes them feel that they need to reciprocate?

The Buddhist texts describe the perfect gift as a gift given with pure intentions to a pure recipient. Being mindful of the gift itself, of the recipient and their circumstances, makes you feel more confident about the gifts you make.

Importantly, be aware of your intentions, especially that you are giving out of generosity, without expectation of reciprocity or even gratitude, and purely for the benefit of the recipient. You will notice that your intentions are often mixed. Acknowledge this ambivalence without judgement.

Focus on the wholesome intentions and resolve to continue cultivating them.

208   Generosity of spirit: Bernie Glassman

Have you ever had Ben & Jerry's Chocolate Fudge Brownie ice cream? You've had Zen ice cream! The brownies used in this ice cream come from the Greyston Bakery in Yonkers, New York. This bakery was founded in 1982 by Bernie Glassman, an American Zen Buddhist teacher who epitomized the virtue of generosity.

Yonkers was a city that had its share of violence, drugs and unemployment. Bernie, as he liked to be called, believed that serving the community was a way to practise Zen and practising Zen was a way of serving the community.

As a rule, Greyston Bakery gave a job to anyone who asked for it, regardless of their status, and provided them with wide-ranging support. Despite this unusually open hiring policy, the bakery was very successful and now has nearly 200 employees. Bernie Glassman believed that every person is trustworthy and capable, demonstrating his generosity of spirit.

How can you show generosity of spirit to those around you? What does it look like when you show generosity of spirit?

209   What's your great gift?

For Buddhists, giving the Buddhist teachings is the greatest gift. This extends to any advice or knowledge that helps us live better and happier lives.

Write about a time when you received such a gift, a piece of advice, or read about a practice or a habit that changed your usual way of thinking. What was the advice you received? Who gave it to you? What made you trust this person (or that book)? How did you implement it? In what ways did it change your thinking or behaviour?

Conversely, write about a time when you shared beneficial advice or knowledge. Describe who you gave it to and how it helped them.

210   Just do it!

Just do it! I challenge you to act on your generous thoughts! Next time you think of a gift, whether a material gift, a gift of attention or time, don't let it pass. Act on it.

Just do it!

CHAPTER 8
LOVING KINDNESS

211　Loving kindness

Loving kindness is closely associated with and naturally leads to compassion. As one cultivates loving kindness, the wish for all beings' wellbeing and happiness, compassion, the desire to relieve their suffering, spontaneously arises. Loving kindness, like compassion, is one of the four *brahma-vihāras* – literally, 'divine dwellings'. It is described in the Buddhist texts as one of four higher meditation states.

In the well-known *Mettā Sutta* (Loving Kindness Sutta), the Buddha urges us to consider all beings with the love a mother has for her only child. The sutta has developed into a common contemporary loving kindness practice to cultivate benevolence and kindness towards all beings.

212　When do you feel loving kindness?

Buddhist texts describe loving kindness as the feeling a mother has for her child, wishing for their wellbeing and happiness. What is loving kindness for you? When, and for whom, do you feel it most strongly?

Describe how you experience it in your daily life in as much detail as you can. Imagine how you can cultivate this feeling in a wider range of settings and what these would be.

213　Blending like milk and water: Anuruddha, Nandiya and Kimbila

At the time of the Buddha, three monks, Anuruddha, Nandiya and Kimbila, lived together in the Gosinga Sāla-tree Wood Park. One day, the Buddha visited them and inquired about their wellbeing, asking specifically how they got along with each other. The three monks, having offered the Buddha a seat and water to rinse his feet, responded that they lived 'in friendship, with mutual appreciation, and without dispute, blending like milk and water, viewing each other with kindly eyes'.

The Buddha, curious (and for our edification), asked them how they succeeded in living in such harmony. They explained that they acted out of loving kindness for each other, both publicly and privately. This included trying to fulfil each other's wishes instead of fulfilling their own and taking responsibility for any chore as and when it arose, rather than leaving it to the others. The Buddha, satisfied, congratulated them and went on his way.

Whenever I am about to protest that I have already done the dishes five times this week, I try to remind myself of the monks from the Gosinga Sāla-tree Wood Park.

214   Try a loving kindness meditation

To cultivate loving kindness, contemporary Buddhists have developed various meditation exercises. Typically, the meditation starts by wishing well to yourself, then your loved ones, and then expands to all beings in the universe, wishing for their wellbeing and happiness. You can experiment with it along these lines.

Find a quiet and relaxed space, sit comfortably but alert. Imagine yourself in a form that is most likely to evoke care and affection, the small child you once were, for example. Mentally wish yourself, 'May I be well, may I be safe, may I be healthy and free from suffering, may I be happy.'

Next, think of someone you love dearly and mentally repeat the same words to them: 'May you be well, may you be safe, may you be healthy and free from suffering, may you be happy.'

Continue for as long as you like, ending with good wishes for the whole world: 'May all beings be well, may all beings be safe, may all beings be healthy and free from suffering, may all beings be happy.'

215   A turtle in the ocean

Have you ever noticed how much more loving you feel when you are happy? One Buddhist practice acknowledges the amazing opportunity that a human life offers. For Buddhists, that opportunity is to become awakened or, in other words, to develop our innate wisdom.

A common analogy compares the extraordinary and rare chance of being alive to the likelihood that a turtle, deep in the ocean, would pass her neck through a ring floating on the ocean's surface if she emerged only once every 100 years. That's how rare a human life is considered to be in Buddhist texts.

In the same way that the Buddhist practice cultivates gratitude for this life, you too can cultivate gratitude for the marvellous opportunity that your life represents.

216   The wise person

The wise person knows the true worth of these four kinds of friends:
the friend who helps and the friend in good and bad times, the friend
who walks the right path, and the friend who gives sympathy, and
they cherish them with care, just like a mother with her dearest child.

The Buddha, *Sigālaka Sutta*, *Dīgha Nikāya*, 31

217   Check in with yourself

How often do you ask a friend or a colleague or even a neighbour, when you notice that they're not their usual self, 'How are you?' and offer help? How often do you do this with yourself?

When you do not feel quite like yourself, take a moment to pause. Take two or three deep breaths, filling your lungs and exhaling slowly and gently. Then check in with yourself. What is the dominant emotion or feeling right now? Where do you feel it the most? How does it feel? Bring a kind and interested awareness to what you are feeling. Give it space to be there. Give yourself the space to experience these feelings and emotions fully.

Maybe you can gently tell yourself 'it's okay' (or words to that effect) to remind yourself that you are willing to allow your experience completely and without judgement.

Experiment with this habit a few times a day, especially when you're feeling strong and disruptive emotions.

218   Heaven and hell

A Buddhist monk visits hell. The people there are seated at long and wide tables facing each other. They are pale and emaciated despite the dishes, heaped high with delicious food, steaming on the table – they hold spoons with handles so long that they cannot use them to feed themselves.

The next day, the same monk visits heaven. There, the beings are seated at the same tables as the beings in hell, but they look happy and satiated – each person is using their long-handled spoon to feed the person sitting across from them.

When we focus only on ourselves, we are in hell. When we take care of each other, we create heaven.

219   What's your spark?

It is not always easy to feel loving or kind towards ourselves or those around us. To help develop loving kindness, Tibetan Buddhists like to remind themselves that, at some point in a past life, everyone has been their mother. But we don't have to focus on our parents – and, in some cases, that wouldn't work at all!

Think about who or what arouses loving kindness for you. Who, or what, sparks feelings of love and care in your heart when you think of them? Is it someone dear to you? Is it a small child? Is it a pet?

Write about how they make you feel and describe how you can bring them to mind to arouse loving kindness towards yourself and others.

220   Ānanda stands up for women's rights

Ānanda was the Buddha's well-beloved attendant, who was greatly admired for his extraordinary memory. It is said that as one of the Buddha's closest disciples and attendant for more than 25 years, he was present for many of the Buddha's teachings and was able to recite them at the first council after the Buddha's death, allowing the teachings to be preserved and transmitted.

Ānanda is renowned for the deep kindness and care he extended to everyone he met. He appears as a gentle soul, who may not be as advanced on the path as the Buddha's other close disciples, Sāriputta and Moggallāna, but his empathy and concern for the suffering of others make him immediately likable and approachable to ordinary people.

He is also celebrated for his support for women. In one well-known episode, he persuaded the Buddha to allow women to be ordained as nuns at a time when women's roles were restricted to marriage and motherhood. Although he was blamed by other monks for his intercession, he had no regret. Today he's still remembered as one who stood up to defend those who were underprivileged and marginalized by society.

221   What you love matters

What do you love? Whom do you love? What do you love doing? What do you love about these things and people? What makes you come alive? Start a practice of intentionally reflecting on what you love.

Daily, as you go about your day, think about what you love about each moment. If you're going to work, what do you love about your work? If you're meeting a colleague or a client, what do you appreciate in them? If you're going for a walk, what do you like about walking and the place where you walk?

By thinking and talking about the things you love, you actively connect with the sources of joy and energy and make them more vivid and vibrant in your life.

P.S. That doesn't mean you have to love it all, but this practice is about recognizing and appreciating the things you *do* love.

222   The house is on fire

We are busy. We have long to-do lists. We make it to bed with many of our to-dos not done. We didn't have the time, the energy or the courage to do them all. Although we have done many things we didn't care much about, it is often the things left undone that are those most important to us.

In the *Lotus Sūtra*, the Buddha compares life to a house on fire in which children are playing, oblivious to their impending doom. *We* are the children. We are oblivious to our impermanence. We are oblivious to what matters most to us.

Live as though your life is on fire! Identify what you care most about and decide to drop all the things that don't actually matter.

223   What are you going through?

The love of our neighbour in all its fulness simply means being able to say, 'What are you going through?'
Simone Weil (1909–1943)

224   Cultivate gratitude

Gratitude has been found to have a beneficial impact not only on people's social life but also on their health. You can develop an attitude of gratitude towards life and the people around you by contemplating what they bring to your life.

You can also expand the circle of who you include in your gratitude. Besides your loved ones and the people who have had a direct impact on your wellbeing, think about the work and efforts of those who make your life much easier to live. Without them, you would have to grow your own food and make your own clothes. You'd have to dispose of your own rubbish, clean your sewers yourself or produce your own electricity.

In every instant, your life is made more comfortable by the work of countless people. Acknowledging our interdependence and feeling grateful is fertile soil for loving kindness.

225   Don't 'phub' your friends

Research has shown that using your smartphone when you are in a social setting – having dinner with friends, visiting relatives or just having coffee with a colleague – has a negative impact on the quality of your experience. Not only will those you're with feel 'phubbed', but they will not enjoy your company as much and *you* will have less fun and be more bored.

Try this challenge: this week or, if you're feeling brave, this whole month, every time you have a social interaction, put your phone away completely. Either turn it off or put it on silent and keep it out of sight. Give your full attention to the present moment, to the people you are with, and to enjoying this time with others.

226   Where is your refuge?

The formal way of becoming a Buddhist is to 'take refuge' in the Three Jewels: the Buddha (the teacher), the Dharma (the teachings) and the Sangha (the Buddhist community). Afterwards, Buddhists usually recite the 'refuge' prayer daily as they make offerings to the Buddha, their teacher, and other bodhisattvas and awakened beings.

When Buddhists take refuge, they recall the role model they seek to emulate, the Buddhist teachings they seek to follow and the community they belong to. These Three Jewels are also a refuge because they are always available to offer insight, support and comfort. They are a source of strength and wisdom and an anchor in stormy and troubled times.

Think about the people who inspire you, the principles that guide you and the community that sustains you: these are your refuge.

Develop a simple way of remembering them regularly.

227   Doing good for others: Hakuin's search for awakening

When the great Japanese Zen master Hakuin Ekaku (1689–1769) was a child in a small town at the foot of Mount Fuji, he heard a visiting monk describe the Buddhist hells in such frightening words that he decided to do everything he could to save himself, including becoming a monk at the age of 15.

He spent many years sitting in meditation, but dejected by his lack of meditative achievement and thinking of giving up the monastic life, he started travelling to visit different masters. During one of these visits, he came across a book on Zen and rededicated himself to being a monk.

He continued to travel to various Zen masters, some of them very harsh and demanding, but although he finally started reaching meditative states of tranquillity when he was 23, he lamented that he could not bring calm and ease into his daily life.

At 31, Hakuin returned to his hometown and was appointed head priest of the temple where he had been ordained. It was only when he was 41 that he finally had a great realization: awakening was found only in doing good for others.

228   Who are your people?

Research shows that one of the most important sources of meaning in our lives comes from our close relationships.

Describe the important relationships in your life. In what ways do these relationships bring you meaning? What do you draw from them? What do you bring to them? Think about ways you can improve and strengthen these relationships.

Be detailed and specific.

229   Click the refresh icon

The Buddhist practice of visualizing bodhisattvas and deities helps the practitioner bring to mind their qualities and attributes, such as the comforting compassion of Avalokiteśvara or the illuminating wisdom of Mañjuśrī.

We can bring this practice into our daily life by recalling the qualities and talents of the people around us, whom we often take for granted. When you deliberately reflect on your loved ones' qualities and how they enrich your life, they will appear bright and fresh to your mind and you will feel energized. It also allows you to cultivate an attitude of gratitude towards them which helps strengthen your relationship.

Take time to contemplate your loved ones' qualities. Visualize how these qualities manifest in their relationship to you in detailed and specific ways. Think of it as clicking the refresh icon!

230   Loving kindness is hard work

A practice of loving kindness that has become very popular is the sitting meditation in which we extend good wishes to people we love dearly, to those we feel more neutral towards, and sometimes even include those we actively feel unfriendly towards.

But loving kindness must go beyond a meditation practice that engages only little of us. Loving kindness is hard work. Loving kindness means that you treat people around you with kindness. You don't need to *feel* the loving part of it, but you need to *act* the kindness part.

What does it mean practically? See people you interact with as full human beings. Give them the benefit of the doubt: assume that their actions are motivated by seeking the goodness in life. As the 14th Dalai Lama reminds us, remember that all people, like you, want to be happy and to avoid suffering.

231   Bright and brilliant

Loving kindness shines forth, bright and brilliant,
just as the morning star shines at dawn, bright and brilliant,
and releases our mind from its fetters.

The Buddha, *Itivuttaka*, 1.27

232   Try non-judging

Our mind is like a pocket courtroom. Wherever we go, whatever we do, we carry it with us. We are constantly judging. Listen to the monologue playing inside your head. Beautiful weather! Oh, no, it's raining again.

I hate this film. I love this song. I can't stand pineapple. More chocolate cake! I made a mistake, I'm so incompetent.

The Buddha described this as two of the three unwholesome roots – the qualities that motivate our actions: greed and aversion. We want more of what we like and we reject what we don't like. The Buddha also explained the third unwholesome root, ignorance or delusion, that undergirds the other two – not understanding that all things are impermanent and subject to change, and ultimately not a source of true contentment and happiness.

Try non-judging. Every time you catch yourself judging anything – the weather, the food, someone, yourself – anything at all, rephrase it as a non-judgemental statement.

233   Connect to the world around you

A sense of connection is crucial to wellbeing. Connection to the place you live in, to its history and geology, to its people, fauna and flora, can be created and strengthened by increasing your knowledge and understanding of how a place has become the place it is today, with its cultural and physical specificities.

Cultivate a habit of exploring and learning about different aspects of your surroundings. Be a tourist or a researcher in your own town or city. As you develop your knowledge about the place and its people, its non-human inhabitants and its vegetation, your connection to the place will deepen and your sense of belonging will intensify.

Soon, all things in your environment will be like old friends that greet you with loving kindness as you walk and drive around.

234   Write your own loving kindness meditation

A popular meditation is based on the *Mettā Sutta*, a canonical Buddhist text on loving kindness. In this text, the Buddha tells his monastic community to develop loving kindness towards all beings in the universe.

There are many contemporary versions, most of which are a variant on wishing wellbeing, safety and happiness to yourself and others.

Write your own version of a loving kindness meditation. What do you wish for yourself, for your loved ones and for the world in general? Be creative!

235 Stoking the spiritual fire: the fire *puja* and *drupchen* ceremonies

The fire *puja* is a fire ritual during which offerings are burned. Fire *pujas* are usually performed in the five cardinal directions (north, south, east, west and centre), which also correspond to the Five Buddha Families.

They are intended to promote healing and pacifying, to eliminate obstacles and foster the growth of all good things, be they in the worldly realm (for example wealth, success, fame, longevity) or in the spiritual realm (for example wisdom and meditative attainments).

Fire *pujas* are always included in *drupchens* – ten-day ceremonies in Tibetan Buddhism, which are led by high-ranking Tibetan Buddhist teachers and include fire *pujas*, ritual music and dances, and sacred mandala painting.

It is believed that participating in such rituals helps remove the negative impact of past actions, and promotes the wellbeing of the participants and of the wider world. In Tibetan lore, it is considered that attending a *drupchen* has the same spiritual benefits as doing a seven-year solitary meditation retreat.

236 Be the friend you want to have

The fact is that we only have real control over what we do, but not over what other people think, feel or do. Once you realize this, you can stop trying to figure out how to relate to others. Instead, you can cultivate the practice of being the friend you want to have. Ask yourself what you want from a friend and *be* that friend.

Do you want a thoughtful and considerate friend? Be thoughtful and considerate to your friends. Do you want a partner that gives you the benefit of the doubt? Give them the benefit of the doubt. Do you want a supportive and understanding co-worker? Be supportive and understanding to your co-workers.

Remember, though – you cannot control what they will feel, think or do. So… do what you do because this is the friend you want to be.

237   You're a hero

When the Covid-19 pandemic hit in early 2020 and the world came to a standstill, many of us realized how dependent we were on the labour of others. When schools, shops, restaurants and cinemas shut down and many of us were encouraged or forced to stay home, some of us still went to work. The nurses, the doctors, the hospital workers, the supermarket workers, the refuse collectors, the electricity infrastructure or road repair workers, to name just a few.

We felt 'all in it' together, but some of us were more 'in it' than others. We created rituals to thank those who went to work and took many risks to serve. In many countries, people opened their windows and clapped or banged pots and pans every evening or once a week to express their gratitude.

As the pandemic went on, we became used to it and the gratitude rituals slowly disappeared. But those who continue providing the services and goods that make life safer, easier and more pleasant don't have to do so. They could just take a break.

The doctor and the dentist could simply stop working. The teachers and waiters, the shopworkers and the nurses could all just decide that it's not worth it. The actors and set workers that make the films and TV shows we enjoy so much, the musicians and artists, they all contribute to a better life.

You contribute to a better life. *You* could decide to stay at home, but when you don't, and you go out there to contribute your piece to the community, you're also a hero.

238 The most difficult task

For one human being to love another, that is perhaps the most difficult of all our tasks, the ultimate, the last test and proof, the work for which all other work is preparation.

Rainer Maria Rilke (1875–1926), *Letters to a Young Poet*

239 Pick up the dropped stitches

Mindfulness uses breath as an anchor for attention because breath is always present. Breathing is, of course, an essential and immediate need. We can live without eating or even drinking, at least for some time, but we cannot live more than a few minutes without breathing.

Breathing marks the beginning and the end of life, and each breath brings us back to the reality of life itself, whether we think about it or not. Each breath is a moment of life. When you focus on the breath, you hold the yarn of life itself, knitted stitch after stitch. Did you drop a stitch? You've missed a moment of life. Drop too many and life starts unravelling.

Mindfulness helps you fix dropped stitches. As you pick up breath after breath, you knit your life back together.

240   Focus on the good

Thousands of years of evolution have primed our brain to focus on what can go wrong. It's a natural and useful feature of the way our attention works, but it can get in the way of appreciating life's goodness. One of the most important Buddhist practices can help correct this tendency: focus on the good.

Today, every time you think of something negative, think about a positive. Every time you are about to say something negative, replace it with something positive. Think about a positive, not just the absence of a negative. For example, I complain a lot when it rains, but rain is good for the vegetation and for replenishing water tables.

Because your experience is what your attention is on moment by moment, when you intentionally focus on the good in your life, your experience becomes good.

Try it for a day, for a month or for ever!

CHAPTER 9
CONTEMPLATION

241   Living and breathing

The basic purpose of Buddhist meditation is to experience the true nature of reality, that all is constantly changing, impermanent, ultimately unsatisfactory and, often, a source of suffering. One aspect of this suffering is that we don't have control over most of what happens – either within or outside us. The Covid-19 pandemic has been a world-shaking reminder of this lack of control.

How do we experience reality? We can observe it, but we quickly get entangled in the many stories of the world outside and inside us. We need to slow down. When we slow down, we can observe what happens in our mind and body – the two are intimately connected.

Simply start by pausing for a moment, right now. Close your eyes. Be aware of where your body is positioned: your feet, your legs, your torso, your arms, your head. Be aware of areas of tension and discomfort. Experience yourself as a living and breathing body. That's all there is to it.

242   What is contemplation?

What is contemplation for you? In this exercise, write about your idea of contemplation – what it means for you and what kinds you find appealing.

Do you prefer to reflect on a religious role model, such as the Buddha or Thich Nhat Hanh, or a more secular example, such as a great artist or activist, or even a friend you admire? Or do you prefer to focus on a supernatural force or presence? Do you enjoy guided meditations or are you more partial to natural sounds?

Consider the qualities that inspire you and that you would like to develop with this practice. Think also about what benefits contemplation can bring – what do you hope they will bring to you?

If you already have a contemplation or meditation practice, what do you like about it? What do you want to keep the same? What do you want to change? If you don't have such a practice, how can you develop one?

243   Cutting through ignorance: Mañjuśrī

Armed with a flaming sword in his right hand and the *Perfection of Wisdom Sūtra* in his left hand, Mañjuśrī, the bodhisattva of wisdom, cuts through ignorance and delusion. Throughout the ages, he appears in various guises – as a beggar, a thief, a gambler – to spiritual masters, ascetics, pilgrims and ordinary people too. Mañjuśrī helps beings and inspires great wisdom, revealing the true nature of reality.

In one story, he appeared as a beggar woman at the door of a temple where there was a celebration. The abbot of the temple gave her food, but the woman kept asking for more, pointing to her children, then her dog and finally her pregnant belly. The abbot, exasperated by the woman's insatiable appetite, tried to send her away, when she revealed herself as Mañjuśrī. The abbot and all those present, finally seeing reality without ignorance and delusion, attained awakening.

The lesson from this story is that we never know when we are encountering a bodhisattva. Every encounter or situation can awaken us to the true nature of reality.

When have you seen Mañjuśrī at work in your life?

244   Arriving home

Do you know the feeling of arriving home after a long day at work or after some time away? That moment when you drop off your luggage or take off your coat and your shoes and exhale as you look around you and *feel* that you have arrived home?

This is the metaphor that meditation teacher Tara Brach uses to explain the practice of bringing back your attention to the present moment, to the internal and external sensations and perceptions occurring right now.

Now is your home. Your experience as it unfolds is your home. When your mind wanders off on a little trip outside of the present moment, bring it back home.

245   How muddy is the water in your glass?

A Buddhist metaphor compares the ordinary mind to muddy water. It is troubled and unclear. As we rush from one thing to another, we keep disturbing the water.

Meditation is the opportunity to leave the muddy water of our mind undisturbed for a little while. With calm and stillness, the mud slowly settles at the bottom, leaving the water pure and clear, our mind tranquil and refreshed. This is what Buddhists call *śamatha*, calm meditation.

Remember that the point is not to judge the mud or get rid of it. The mud is part of our life and, as the Zen teacher Thich Nhat Hanh was fond of saying, 'No mud, no lotus.'

So don't judge the mud, or your mind or your thoughts and feelings, but let them settle gently, so that you can enjoy a moment of quiet and rest. And a glass of clear water.

246   Life is not brief

Life is not brief, but we waste a lot of it. Life is long enough, and we have been given enough time for the highest achievements if only we used it well. When we waste our life on useless and mindless activities, it's only upon death's arrival, that we realize that life has gone and we did not know it.

Seneca (1–65 CE), *On the Briefness of Life*

247   Pause and breathe

Take a moment. Pause and breathe.

Are you late? Are you caught up in the morning rush to get out the door? Pause and breathe. Just a breath.

Close your eyes. Feel your feet grounded. Feel the air on your face. Feel your hands. Inhale to the count of five, feeling the air as it enters your nostrils, travels down to your lungs and inflates your chest and belly. Hold to a count of five, focusing on the sensations of holding the breath. Exhale slowly to a count of five, feeling how the body relaxes. Hold to a count of five as your body settles.

How do you feel?

248   Insight meditation

Vipassana – or insight meditation – is the form of meditation that has most deeply influenced the development of mindfulness in the last few decades, especially in North America and Europe. Its fundamental techniques are drawn from the *Mahāsatipaṭṭhāna Sutta* of the Pāli canon (the texts of Theravāda Buddhism, the form of Buddhism practised predominantly in South and South-East Asia).

These techniques apply mindfulness to the body, feelings, emotions and thoughts and, finally, to the basic physical and mental components of our experience. This consists, essentially, in simply noting what is present in the body and mind, without judgement.

Eventually, the text explains how to analyse the nature of our experience in terms of the Four Noble Truths of Buddhism. In contemporary secular versions of this meditation, this last step focuses on recognizing and accepting the transient nature of our experience and the uncertainty of all things.

Have you ever tried it?

249   What are your recollections?

A very common traditional Buddhist contemplative practice is the 'recollections' during which a Buddhist contemplates the Buddha, his teachings and his community of followers, as well as the virtues they embody such as moral conduct and generosity.

Taken together, these recollections constitute a role model, a guidebook with examples of the virtues Buddhists seek to cultivate and a framework for their life goals and daily behaviours.

Write about your role models and about inspiring examples of the virtues you want to develop. What do you find inspiring about them? How do they exemplify the virtues you have chosen for yourself? How can you emulate them in your own life?

250   Meditating in the forest: Upāsikā Kee Nanāyon

As a child, Kee Nanāyon knew that she did not want the traditional lifestyle of a Thai woman. She was determined to spend her time meditating and studying the Buddha's teaching. Born in 1901, in Rajburi, a town west of the capital city of Bangkok, Kee Nanāyon grew up in a shopkeeping family. When she got older, she started her own shop to support her elderly father, but when she was not minding the shop, she was meditating or reading Buddhist texts.

After her father's death, she, along with her aunt and uncle, withdrew to a small forest retreat where they spent their time meditating and studying the Buddhist teachings. They lived off what they could gather from the surrounding forest and slept in an abandoned meditation hall. Gradually, other people came to join them and Kee Nanāyon started guiding them in their practice. As her reputation grew, many women joined the small community, which eventually became established as Khao Suan Luang.

For Upāsikā (devout lay woman) Kee Nanāyon, contemplation is all there is to the practice of the Buddhist path. Only when you give up attachment to results can you achieve true realization and a clear awareness of the true nature of things.

251   Take a forest bath

The practice of forest bathing (*shinrin-yoku*) was developed in the 1980s as a response to the stress of living in the overcrowded cities of modern Japan.

Qin Li, the head of the Japanese Society of Forest Medicine, has spent many years researching the therapeutic effects of forest bathing and explains that spending time in forests, or other natural environments, has beneficial health effects, such as reducing stress, anxiety, depression and anger. It can also help improve cardiovascular and metabolic health, and even strengthen the immune system.

Forest bathing is simply the practice of walking slowly and in silence in a wooded area, being fully present to the sounds, smells and sights around you. If a forest is not easily accessible, spending time in a local park, or even having green plants in your work and living environments, has been shown to have a positive impact on our mood.

Will you give it a try?

252   Bring the attention back

Meditation is often mistakenly believed to be an attempt to empty the mind, but it is almost the opposite of that. In the case of the contemporary form of mindfulness, meditation is observing, recognizing and fully accepting every perception, sensation, feeling, emotion and thought that goes through our mind.

The mind's job, so to speak, is to produce thoughts, and it is very good at it. Mindfulness is your opportunity to see the mind at work. You bring your attention to what is happening in your mind. You observe the sensations that arise: knees hurting, cheek itching, back tensing. Oh, that knee really hurts! The feelings that follow: rejection, restlessness, agitation. And the thoughts that pick up the conversation: I am getting old. I need to exercise more regularly. I don't have time. This project is due in two days. Oh no, I forgot to call the dentist.

Before you know it, you are somewhere else altogether. But you keep bringing back your attention to the present moment. Whether you are sitting on a cushion or in a train on your morning commute, that is mindfulness: noticing the mind wandering and bringing it back to here and now.

253   The limitless release of the mind

Meditate... with a mind filled with loving kindness,... with a mind filled with compassion,... with a mind filled with joy,... with a mind filled with equanimity, with abundance and generosity, without limits and without hostility or ill will. This is called the limitless release of the mind.

The Buddha, *Mahāvedalla Sutta, Majjhima Nikāya*, 43

254   Touch something

Did you know that there are many more sensory receptors on your fingertips than most other places in your body?

Try this exercise. Pick something with texture: a piece of cloth, a textured stress ball, a chunk of tree bark. Close your eyes. Now, touch your object. Pay attention to its size, temperature, weight and texture – how it feels under your fingers. Small or large? Warm or cool? Heavy or light? Tight or fuzzy? Rough or smooth? Feel the grooves and ridges, the bumps and dips, the lines and curves. Be fully present to the sensations in your fingers.

In moments of stress or restlessness, you can use this exercise to ground you in the moment.

255   Meditate!

This is a challenge for you to meditate. I know what you will say – you don't know how, you don't know when, you don't know why. Mostly, you will argue that you don't have the time.

Here, meditate three minutes a day. Choose a time – maybe when you just wake up in the morning or just before you go to bed at night. Sit on a chair or on a cushion. Set a timer for three minutes and for *three* minutes breathe consciously. You don't need to slow down your breathing or exaggerate it. Simply breathe in and out, letting the breath move naturally. Focus on where the sensations of breathing are strongest – maybe at the nostrils where the air comes in and out, or in the shoulders or the chest as they rise and fall, or in the belly as it expands and relaxes. When your mind wanders, bring it back to the sensations of the breath.

That's it! That's three minutes.

256   The *keisaku*

Imagine that every time you get distracted you are brought back to attention by a more or less gentle whack on the shoulder.

In the Japanese practice of *zazen* (sitting meditation), it is customary for a meditation hall monitor to hold a *keisaku*, a thin wooden stick. The monitor uses the *keisaku* to strike the meditator on the shoulders, either at the request of the meditator themselves or at their own discretion.

When a meditator feels sleepy, distracted or restless, they bow their head to request the *keisaku*. Or when the monitor sees a slouching or sleepy meditator, they'll stand behind them, gently touch them with the stick to warn them and when the meditator bows and presents their shoulder, strike them, rousing them back to alertness and concentration.

In what ways do you awaken your attention and focus as you go about your day?

257   Try meditation journalling

Journalling can help us process events, emotions, feelings and thoughts. As we put pen to paper, we externalize our thoughts and feelings and *de-fuse* from them – that is, we realize that they are not us and we are not them. Journalling can also help shed light on habitual processes and issues. Likewise, meditation journalling can help us identify recurring themes and patterns in our meditation practice.

Like everything in mindfulness practice, meditation journalling should be non-judgemental – and non-judgemental about the judgements bound to occur. Write about the thoughts, feelings and questions that arise in your meditation or contemplation practice. Note how you feel – again without judgement.

The point is to explore your experience as it is and learn from it.

258   Time and space

In Tibetan Buddhism, dedicated practitioners, usually members of the monastic community, may decide to do a three-year retreat. For three years, they step away from the ordinary concerns of daily life and focus entirely on spiritual practice. They spend most of their time meditating, waking up at three or four in the morning and sitting in meditation for many hours every day.

Retreatants often say that it is not the physical challenges of retreat that are most difficult to overcome but the psychological ones. Because they are not distracted by the demands of daily life, retreatants must engage fully with their minds, their thoughts and their emotions. Many see this as an opportunity to deepen and strengthen their spiritual practice in a way that would be impossible outside of retreat. Some say that the three-year retreat makes them better able to be of help to others when they come out.

You may not be able (or even want) to do a three-year retreat, but when do you find time and space to resource yourself?

259   Be like water

According to Japanese Zen master Hakuin Ekaku (1686–1769), the nature of all beings is Buddha, just as the nature of ice is water. For Hakuin, the difference between a Buddha and ordinary beings is the same as that between water and ice.

He believed that we all have innate wisdom, and it is just a matter of letting the limitations and obstructions of a hurried and constricted life fall away through seeing things as they are, without judgement, grasping or rejection.

See the spring come and the ice melt. Let the sun of mindfulness melt the ice of your heart and let the water of awakening and innate wisdom run clear and pure.

260   Three deep breaths

Many forms of meditation centre on the breath as the basic focus of attention. Some aim to control the breath in specific ways; others simply to use it as an anchor for the attention. The breath is always with us, so it is easy and convenient to reach for it whenever we want to be mindful.

It also brings us back in touch with the body and bodily sensations (which we too often ignore during our daily activities) and grounds us into the present moment – you can only ever take a breath now.

In many traditions, breath is understandably associated with the energy of life. Our life starts when we breathe our first breath and ends with the last.

Physiologically, studies have shown that slow breathing helps regulate the nervous system and impacts positively on cardiovascular health and autonomic function (all the stuff that happens outside of conscious control, such as your heart beating).

Now, take three deep breaths.

261   Milarepa sees all this

This is the Rock of Enlightenment, solitary and peaceful...
Surrounded by snowy mountains.
Across are leafy trees,
Below are blooming meadows.
Bees hum around fragrant blooming lotuses,
And, in lakes and along streams, cranes bend their neck, content...
I, Milarepa the yogin, see all this...
And meditate on these sense objects, like water in a mirage.

Milarepa (1028–1123), *One Hundred Thousand Songs*

262   Be curious

Be curious about your emotions and feelings.

When a strong emotion or feeling arises, pause a moment. How does it feel? Focus on your body, not on what's happening in your mind. Where is the sensation associated with the emotion located in your body? What shape does it have? Is it warm or cool? Is it tight or diffuse? Is it tranquil or agitated? Is it becoming stronger or weaker as you explore it?

See if you can breathe through it and give it the space it needs.

263   Visualizing a deity

In Vajrayāna Buddhism, a common form of practice is the visualization of bodhisattvas and buddhas. Bodhisattvas are not very different from buddhas in their activities and characteristics, although they are often considered to be more actively involved in worldly affairs as they endeavour to help all beings on their path to awakening.

The practice starts with visualizing the deity with all the attributes and ornaments that are symbols of their spiritual qualities. For example, the sword of Mañjuśrī cuts through ignorance and the lotus of Avalokiteśvara represents his infinite compassion. Eventually, advanced (and initiated) meditators visualize themselves as a bodhisattva.

It is believed that as you visualize yourself as the deity and contemplate their qualities, you will eventually manifest these qualities yourself. Psychologically, this makes sense. As we deeply reflect on spiritual and moral qualities, we will be more inclined to embody them in our daily lives than if we never think of them.

What do you think?

264   How to be positive

We tend to see things in stark contrasts – something is good or bad, useful or useless, happy or sad – but the fact is that most things have many sides.

In this exercise, write about a challenging situation that you view negatively, and instead of focusing on the negative aspects, focus on its positive aspects, or what could turn out to be positive.

Be creative here, and don't hesitate to go out on a limb. For example, let's say that you didn't get the promotion you were hoping for, or you feel stuck at work. What could be positive about *that*? Maybe it forces you to make an honest inventory of your skills and shortcomings. Maybe it helps you explore other professional avenues. Maybe it helps you develop positive strategies to deal with disappointments and setbacks.

Whatever the case may be, be as inventive as you can and even use humour when possible.

265   Where is your flashlight?

Neuroscientist Amishi Jha compares one form of attention – focused attention – to a flashlight. She explains that this form of attention shines a sustained and focused beam of light on the thing we are looking at, literally or metaphorically.

This form of attention is easily distracted away from its object by external or internal disruptions. For example, the ping of an incoming message or a sudden rush of emotion will immediately and irresistibly yank our flashlight away.

We cannot prevent this from happening, but we can control what happens next. We can either keep our flashlight on the new object presented by the interference: check our phone, or get immersed in the intrusive emotion, for example. *Or*, we can bring the flashlight back to where we want it as soon as we've noticed that it has moved.

Mindfulness is precisely this process of noticing where your flashlight is and returning it to where you want it to be.

266   Don't get on that train!

Many meditation teachers tell us to think of our mind as the sky and our thoughts and emotions as clouds in the sky.

I don't know about you, but my mind is nothing like a tranquil sky in which a few clouds parade about slowly. It is more like a train station. It's busy and crowded. My thoughts are like trains arriving and leaving relentlessly. My emotions are like people rushing to the platforms to get on a train or disembarking with their luggage amid the rush-hour crowd.

My meditation, then, is really about watching the commotion without getting on any train or following anyone out of the train station. I see myself sitting under the central clock and watching what is going on around me. My job is to stay where I am.

What is meditation for you?

267   Remember: you will die

Mindfulness of death is a practice found in many traditions around the world – think about the classical and medieval custom of *memento mori* evoked in the title. In Buddhism, a formal practice of contemplation of death takes the meditators through a series of exercises in which they contemplate what happens to the body after death.

Historically, some meditators took this contemplation further and, in fact, went to meditate in charnel grounds where bodies are cremated. What seems at first sight a morbid inclination – reminding ourselves that we, and all those we love, *will* die – can actually help us appreciate the present moment more intensely and avoid taking it for granted. Without sitting in a charnel ground to watch a body decompose.

268   Mind is no other

I came to realize clearly that mind is no other than mountains, rivers, the great wide earth and everything in it.

Dōgen (1200–1253)

269   Change the programme

Do you sometimes get trapped in your own mind? A thought, a feeling, a memory arises and, before you know it, you're listening to the programme on your inner radio. Sometimes the programme is a good one – you're daydreaming about success or an upcoming holiday. Sometimes the programme is a disaster report, blaring that you're a failure and nobody loves you. Whatever the inner radio is playing, you get hooked on it.

But you don't have to. It's just a radio programme. You can change it. Look outside of yourself. What's around you? What does it look like? Are you inside or outside? What's the furniture like? The people? The plants? Cars? Buildings?

Describe it to yourself mentally. For example: 'There is a lady with a small dog. She wears a blue cardigan and red trousers. There is a small grey car driving slowly along the road. There is a wooden chair with a black cushion on the seat.'

You get the drift. The point is not to get rid of your inner radio, that's impossible. You're just changing the programme, gently but firmly.

270   Not the story in your mind

One of the aims of Buddhist calm meditation is to cultivate equanimity, the capacity to accept all things with calm and forbearance. A metaphor in Buddhist texts compares equanimity with the rain that falls on everything and everyone without preference or aversion. Equanimity challenges us to tolerate discomfort and irritation and to let go of desires and cravings.

Develop equanimity in your daily life by recognizing when you are experiencing hostility or desire towards something or someone.

Accept the emotions that the situation triggers, as they are, without judging them or acting on them. If you feel pulled by the necessity to act on them, examine these thoughts too, without judgement. Focus on how they feel in your body. Not the story in your mind.

CHAPTER 10

KNOWLEDGE

271   Like the Kalāmas

In the *Sutta to the Kalāmas*, the Buddha advises the clan of the Kalāmas that they should not accept what they are told, whether it's tradition, scripture, teachings, hearsay or rumour, without evaluating it first. They should ponder each statement or recommendation carefully and ascertain for themselves whether it is true or not. Most importantly, the Buddha says, they should ask themselves whether following the advice will lead to their wellbeing and happiness.

Likewise, some contemporary Buddhist teachers advise us to reflect on our consumption of all media – Hollywood films, fiction, news, video games and social media – and ask ourselves: What does this bring me? Does it contribute to my wellbeing? Does it contribute to my becoming a better person?

Like the Kalāmas, ask yourself what makes you happy and content. Reflect on what you hear and see, and whether it serves your purpose or not. If it does, accept it. If not, let it be.

272   What is knowledge?

In Buddhism, knowledge is the fundamental understanding of the true nature of reality, that all things are impermanent, changing and ultimately unsatisfactory. Buddhists generally consider that, from a spiritual perspective, everything else is knowledge insofar as it helps realizing this truth about the nature of reality.

Spend a moment writing about what spiritual knowledge means for you. What qualities does it have? What does it comprise? And, crucially, what does it help you realize and cultivate?

273   Sharing knowledge: Sāriputta

When the Buddha learned that Sāriputta and Moggallāna, his two chief disciples, had passed away, he stared at the monks assembled around him and lamented, 'This assembly appears to me empty now that Sāriputta and Moggallāna have attained final awakening. This assembly was not empty for me earlier, and I had no concern for where they were.'

Sāriputta was renowned for his understanding of Buddhist doctrines' finer points. Many significant suttas are attributed to him and he is often described teaching monks, outlining the most complex concepts of Buddhist philosophy, or explaining Buddhist psychology.

In one of these suttas, Sāriputta compares the spiritual path with 'good friendship, good companionship, and good comradeship' presaging the Buddha's sorrow at his death.

For Sāriputta, being a good friend meant sharing his knowledge and understanding of the Buddhist teachings with his companions, an endeavour that he pursued and embodied in his life.

274   The conditions of happiness are already here

Zen master Thich Nhat Hanh (1926–2022) liked to tell his students that the conditions for happiness are already present. He encouraged us to look at all the things we can be grateful for, here, right now, and to make a practice of not taking anything for granted. The small things like the blue of the sky, or the refreshing rain, or the big things like good health, or the presence of loved ones, or personal safety.

Remember, before the Covid-19 pandemic, we took for granted going out to a restaurant or the cinema, or taking public transport, or kissing and hugging. Practise being aware of the conditions of happiness in your life right now.

Practise as though they could disappear any instant. They can.

275 What's your reality like?

What is the world really like? We think we have a good grasp on reality and that what we perceive is the way things really are. Buddhist psychology challenges this belief. It tells us that reality is what we make of our perceptions. Our senses perceive and experience sensations – light and shapes, sounds, touch sensations (texture, pressure, temperature), tastes and smells. Our mind perceives and experiences thoughts, feelings and emotions.

Out of these sense perceptions, and based on our experiences and our current mood, we create our reality.

Practising mindfulness helps you notice your mental processes *without* creating a reality out of them. Sound is sound, light is light, touch is touch, a thought is a thought, a feeling is a feeling. It may be pleasant, unpleasant or neutral. That's all there is to it.

P.S. Note that, in Buddhist psychology, the mind is one of the senses – interestingly, modern psychology is now developing an understanding of mind processes very similar to those already described in Buddhist texts composed over 2,000 years ago.

276 When this is

When this is, that comes to be.
When this arises, that arises.
When this does not exist, that does not come to be.
When this ceases, that ceases.
The Buddha, *Mahātanhāsankhaya Sutta, Majjhima Nikāya*, 38

277 Create memories

Do you sometimes realize that you have no idea what was just said? We all do. The mind wanders away from the present moment and gets caught up in a world of its own making.

When we are immersed in our thoughts, we are, in a very real way, not present. Not only does it leave us feeling dissociated from our lives, it also stops us from creating memories of these moments. Even when our body is here, if our brain is not processing what is happening around us, we are wherever our attention is, and we will have little or no recollection of the moment.

A mindful habit is to experience the moment intentionally by using all your senses. Pay attention to the colour of the sky, the birdsongs, the fragrance of the wet earth after the rain, the feel of a wet leaf under your fingers.

The moment will be brighter and more likely to become a memory.

278 Two truths

A difficult concept in Buddhist philosophy is that of the two truths. Conventional truth is the truth of our everyday reality. For example, that we are separate beings that exist independently of each other may be accepted as a conventional truth. The ultimate truth is that we are not separate at all but, rather, fundamentally and inextricably dependent.

Everything we are right now depends not only on our past but also on the existence of myriad other human and non-human beings, and on the natural world.

On a conventional level, it is fine and useful to see ourselves as independent agents, but, on the ultimate level, recognizing our interdependence and inherent connection changes our perspective on our place in the universe.

How does this play out in your life?

279   Find the spaciousness

According to the Buddha, the main reason for our mental anguish is delusion, a deep misunderstanding of the true nature of reality. We see ourselves, people, objects and situations as solid and constant. We don't realize that all things, ourselves included, are in a constant flow of change. Instead, we grasp at them as though they were unchanging and permanent.

Take a moment, and a pen, and write down everything you can remember that you used to like and no longer do. Similarly, write down everything you used to dislike and now enjoy. What conclusions do you draw from this exercise about your present likes and dislikes?

Dwell in the spaciousness and freedom that this opens up.

280   Study without delay: Jetsün Khandro Rinpoche

Khandro Rinpoche believes that there are no greater friends than humour and patience in difficult times. Rinpoche (the precious one) was born Tsering Paldrön in 1967 in the monastery founded in Kalimpong, India, by her father, the head of the Nyingma school of Tibetan Buddhism, after he had fled Tibet.

In the Tibetan tradition, it is believed that great teachers reincarnate time after time and Rinpoche was recognized as such a reincarnation of eminent past teachers. Rinpoche is one of the few female Tibetan Buddhist teachers, and she is a strong advocate for women's religious education. In 1993, she established the Samten Tse Retreat Center in India, where Tibetan nuns can study and practise.

Rinpoche draws from all four Tibetan schools of Buddhism and builds on the nineteenth-century ecumenical Rimé movement. She has also received teachings from many accomplished masters, such as Dilgo Khyentse Rinpoche and the 14th Dalai Lama.

Khandro Rinpoche emphasizes the importance of studying the Dharma with persistence and without delay. What, in your life, should you do with persistence and without delay?

281   What's the story behind the story?

Being mindful of emotions is challenging. When someone pushes our buttons, we react before we know it and we find ourselves embroiled in churning emotions. Mindfulness can help us deal with these reactions.

Try this practice. When you are in a comfortable and safe space, bring to mind a difficult relationship. Ask yourself, what is the story behind the story? What do I believe about this relationship? About this person in the relationship? About myself in the relationship? Where does it hurt? Where does the anger come from?

Bring these feelings and emotions to your awareness and the stories behind them. How do they feel in the body? What sensations do they evoke? How different would the relationship be if you didn't believe these stories?

Is there an opening there for you to let go of the stories? There is no need to judge. See them as what they are: feelings and thoughts that arise, linger and pass on. Thank them for trying to be helpful. Then, set them free.

282   Know thyself

Mindfulness requires self-knowledge. Most often, we seek to develop our mindfulness because we feel stuck in one area of our lives, or because we experience difficulties, or even great suffering. Basically, we want something to change. But the aim of mindfulness is not to get rid of our 'problems' or to achieve a better version of oneself.

Mindfulness is the *full* acceptance of who we are and of our circumstances in *this* moment. This cannot be stressed enough: being mindful is allowing what is to be what it is with an attitude of kindness and acceptance. This does not mean that you cannot seek to change it, but before you can change it, it is necessary to accept it as it is without judgement, blame, shame or hostility.

How would that feel for you?

283   Leather enough

Where would there be leather enough to cover the entire world? With just the leather of my sandals, it is as if the whole world were covered. Likewise, I am unable to control external phenomena, but I can control my own mind. What need is there to control anything else?

Śāntideva (685–763 CE), *Bodhicaryāvatāra*

284   Name your emotions

In moments of stress or strong emotions, the habit of naming what is happening in your mind and body can help create space between you and the unsettling swirl of perceptions, sensations, feelings, thoughts and memories. You can practise in moments of calm so that you are better prepared when disruptive emotions occur.

First, ground yourself, for example by taking a few deep breaths, or feeling the sensation of your feet planted on the ground. Then, observe the sensations, feelings and thoughts occurring in your body and mind and name them. 'There is tension.' 'There is restlessness.' 'There is anger.' 'There is fear.' Nothing more.

This habit helps you realize that you are not your thoughts and emotions. They are like clouds in a sky. They come and they go.

285   Bring your mind and body together

To be fully present, we must learn how to be with our body. Mindfulness starts with mindfulness of the body.

Where is your body in space? Do you feel the air against your cheeks? The seat under your bottom? The ground under your feet? How does your body feel? Is there tension? Feel the area around your eyes, your brow, your jaw. Is it tense? Is it relaxed? Try smoothing the brow, softening the eyes, loosening the jaw.

What about your neck and shoulders? Your back? Your abdomen? Is there any tightness? Fluttering? Twisting? Breathe into it and try to relax any area where there is tension, discomfort or pain. Can you feel your legs? Your feet and toes? Are they warm? Cool? Comfortable? Twitchy?

Today, bring your mind and your body together every time you become aware of an emotion or a sensation.

286   Delusion

Yale professor of psychology and cognitive scientist Laurie Santos, in her online *Science of Happiness* class, explains that we seek happiness in all the wrong places.

The high-paying career? You won't find happiness there. The good grades or glowing promotion? Nope. The beautiful house or hip apartment in a chic neighbourhood? Not even there. Research shows that most of the things we think will bring us happiness in fact don't.

More than 2,000 years ago, the Buddha called this fundamental misunderstanding of the source of happiness 'delusion', the basic ignorance of the true nature of reality. When we see material, external things as the source of long-lasting happiness, we are deluded.

On the one hand, these things are not permanent and unchanging, and their appeal will fade. On the other hand, you are not permanent and unchanging, and the things you want when you're 20 are not the same as those you want when you're 60.

When you remind yourself of these changes, you start tearing the veil of delusion and seeing what truly brings you happiness.

287 What do you feel?

What do you feel right now? Write down everything you feel, from the physical sensations of your hand holding the pen, your feet on the floor, your bottom on the chair, to the emotions you are experiencing.

Try to be specific and detailed. How does the chair feel? Is it soft? Hard? Comfortable? Uncomfortable? Is the pen smooth or rough? Round or hexagonal? Are you feeling happy or joyful? Sad or nostalgic? Angry or irritated? Are these sensations and feelings pleasant, unpleasant or neutral?

If you have a feeling of like or dislike towards your feelings or sensations, note that too. Try not to get into the 'story', just write about what is present in your world right now, without judgement, and when there is judgement, note that too – without judgement.

Now go and grab a pen!

288 Is your cup full?

Sometimes knowledge gets in the way of truly knowing.

The nineteenth-century Zen master Nan-in gave this lesson to a university professor who wanted to know about Zen. After the customary courtesies, the professor asked Nan-in to teach him about Zen. Nan-in remained silent and instead, served the professor tea. He filled the cup to the brim and continued pouring. As the cup overflowed and the tea spilled, the professor, confused, called out to his host to stop. 'The cup is full,' he shouted.

Nan-in looked at him and said, 'You are like this cup. You are full of theories and assumptions. How can I teach you Zen unless your cup is empty?'

How full is *your* cup?

289   Ultimate truth

When Buddhist philosophy differentiates between conventional and ultimate truths, it is not saying that everyday reality does not really exist. It is saying that what we think is important right now may ultimately not be that important. Ten years from now or even a few days or hours from now, we might even wonder why we ever thought it was.

Nurture a perspective-taking practice. When you are confronting a difficult situation, or are feeling irritated or even angry, take a moment to breathe deeply and, at least mentally, remove yourself from the situation.

Ask yourself, 'What will I feel about this in 20 years from now? Will I care about it? How will I wish I had dealt with it?' If that doesn't help, think about a similar occasion in the past – one that you are truly over and done with – and reflect on how you feel about it now.

Realize that, ultimately, most things are relatively unimportant and not worth your energy and time.

290   Leave the raft behind

In the *Alagaddūpama Sutta*, the Buddha compares his teachings to a raft. In the same way that a raft is useful to get across a river or an ocean, the teachings are useful to get to the other side of the ocean of suffering. Once the shore is reached, the raft must be abandoned, otherwise it becomes an inconvenient and useless burden. Likewise, the teachings should not be held for their own sake and become dogmas.

Think of your goals in the same way. They provide a useful impetus for you to give a direction to your life, but they should not be considered rigidly. Just like the raft, they must be dropped or reformulated when they no longer serve.

Are there goals that you are holding on to that would be best released?

291   *Nirvāṇa* is right here

Truly, is anything missing now? *Nirvāṇa* is right here, before our eyes.

> This very place is the Lotus Land,
> This very body, the Buddha.
>
> Hakuin Ekaku (1686–1769)

292   Get your body moving

Because our mind is inextricably linked to our body, engaging in movement can help reset the mind when we are feeling helpless or powerless. Helplessness is the feeling that no matter what we do, we won't be able to solve the problem, get out of a situation, or be of help to others. This feeling causes stress and, over the long term, can also cause depression.

One way to alleviate the feeling of helplessness is to act right now, right here. When a circumstance arises in which you feel helpless, do something. Go for a walk or a run, do a dance routine, fold the laundry, do the dishes, build a bookcase.

Whatever it is, get your body moving! The problem itself may not be solved, but by engaging your body, you are telling your mind that you are not helpless.

293   Enjoyment is not the same as happiness

Enjoyment is not the same as happiness, although it is certainly part of it. When we confuse enjoyment with happiness, we often end up not being very happy.

True happiness, the kind that makes us feel deeply satisfied with how we live our life on a day-to-day basis, requires a sense of meaning beyond simple enjoyment. That meaning arises when we are connecting with something greater than ourselves.

This is what Buddhists do when they share the merit of a good action. They connect their actions with something greater than themselves by dedicating the benefit of their actions for the welfare of all beings.

How do your actions bring meaning to your life? How do they connect you to others and to something greater?

294   Experience alternate realities

In this writing exercise, try experiencing being someone else. For example, choose an instance in which you disagree with someone. Choose an issue that is not too emotionally charged, but where there are still clear differences of opinion.

Now, instead of focusing on why you hold the opinion you do, imagine being the other person. What do they perceive? How do they understand the issue? What in their personal story leads them to feel the way they do? How does the issue affect them differently from you? Where does their understanding diverge from or agree with yours? Are there ways in which you could come to see their perspective more sympathetically? What would it take?

What have you learned about the issue and about yourself in this process?

295   Song of the ultimate truth

Here, then, is a song on ultimate truth:
Thunder, lightning, and clouds
Emerge out of the sky,
And into the sky they dissolve...
Honey, harvest, and fruits
Emerge out of the earth,
And into the earth they dissolve.
Forests, flowers, and leaves,
Emerge out of the mountain,
And into the mountain they dissolve.

Milarepa (1028–1123), *One Hundred Thousand Songs*

296   Where food comes from

Before you start eating, stop for a moment. Observe your food. Ask yourself: Where does it come from? Who planted and harvested it? Who packed and transported it? Who built the roads and the trucks that carried it to where you bought it? Where did the materials for the roads and trucks come from? Where were they mined, processed and assembled? Who unloaded the trucks and shelved the food? Who prepared it for you to eat today?

Think about the many thousands of people who worked so that you can eat. Without their work, you would not be able to eat today. Imagine their lives. How similar or different do you think they are from yours? What about their hopes and aspirations?

Think about the interconnectedness between all human beings on this planet. Once we start unpacking the myriad components that make up a simple tomato, we realize we are connected to the whole universe in a very real way.

297   You don't see what you see

Modern cognitive science agrees with Buddhist psychology that when we perceive a thing, we don't actually perceive it as it is. Our perception is shaped by experience, knowledge and preconceptions. And that's a good thing too! We need to be able to recognize things immediately to be able to function on a daily basis.

But this can be (and often is) problematic when our preconceptions prevent us from seeing what is there. What we know and what we expect interfere with reality and this can have disastrous consequences.

One example is implicit bias, our unconscious tendency to impose certain traits and attributes on people of different ethnic, racial and national groups, instead of seeing them as individuals. This leads to discrimination, injustice and even severe harm or death.

When you expand your mindfulness, you become more aware of these tendencies and can address them in ways that are more consistent with your values.

298   Shower with the world

The shower is usually the time when we can finally be alone. Well, not so! Next time, when you turn on the shower, think about where the water comes from and how it connects you with the entire world not only today but in the past and future as well.

As you wash yourself, think that this water was present when dinosaurs roamed the Earth and will still be here for our descendants. It has travelled around the world as a cloud, bathed worshippers in the Ganges and in Mecca. It has satiated the thirst of birds and insects, and served as the home of fish, sea lions and frogs.

Reflect on how fortunate you are to have this fresh and clean water to wash yourself with today. Leave enough for those who will come tomorrow.

299   Be a lake

A Zen story tells you to imagine drinking a cup of water in which you have poured a spoonful of salt. Unpleasant, isn't it? Next, imagine pouring the spoonful of salt into a large, clear and pure lake. Would you notice the salt now?

When you encounter irritations, annoyances and discomforts in the course of the day, you can choose to be small like the glass of water or wide and spacious like the lake.

300   Reset your reference point

One of the things that prevents us from enjoying life is the psychological process of habituation. We just get used to the good stuff and after a while it doesn't feel so good anymore. That doesn't apply only to mind-altering substances like alcohol and other drugs, but also to romantic love or to how we feel about a great job or a new gadget.

To slow or prevent this process of habituation, we can reset our reference point by remembering how we felt before. The more you like someone or something, the more you want to remember how it felt before that person or thing was in your life. This resets your reference point in the present and counteracts the effects of habituation.

Pick someone or something you enjoy in your present life and recall how life was before, or imagine what it would be like if they weren't in your life right now. What would you miss?

Do this exercise whenever you feel that you are taking someone or something for granted.

CHAPTER 11

PATIENCE

301　How to be patient

On one occasion, the Buddha's cousin, Devadatta, intent on taking the Buddha's place at the helm of the Buddhist community, had tried to kill him by dropping a boulder on him. Fortunately, he only succeeded in injuring the Buddha's foot. The pain, however, was severe, the story goes, and the Buddha lay down to rest.

Māra, the personification of all evils in the Buddhist texts, visited the Buddha and taunted him. Not only was the Buddha lazing about, Māra jeered, but he let Devadatta's attack pass without retribution. The Buddha remained unperturbed at Māra's abuse, and Māra left, seething with frustration.

Patience is this quality of remaining unflustered by adverse events and facing difficulties, small or big, with a calm and composed mind. It is one of the ten perfected virtues of a Buddha, and a virtue that most Buddhists seek to develop.

Who do you know who can display the patience of a Buddha?

302　What is patience for you?

Time to write! What is patience for you? What are you patient with? What are you impatient with? What physical sensations, emotions, feelings and thoughts are present when you are patient? What physical sensations, emotions, feelings and thoughts are present when you are impatient?

Describe in detail how the virtue of patience plays out in your life.

303　Practise patience

Next time you are waiting in traffic, or waiting for the bus or the train, practise patience. Don't pull out your phone, or any other distraction. Sit there and *be* fully there. Don't check the time.

Observe life around you. What's the weather like? What colour is the sky? What vegetation can you see? What buildings? Who can you see? Observe impartially and without judgement. What is happening in your mind? Are you wondering how much longer you need to wait? Observe this non-judgementally as well.

When you are patient, you are present to your life, moment by moment. Remember: that's all there is to it.

Look! The traffic is moving again.

304 Patience and perseverance: Dhammananda's fight for the Thai nuns

Bhikkhunī Dhammananda's strength shines through her soft voice and gentle demeanour. For the past 40 years, she has been defending women's right to seek higher ordination in the Theravāda Buddhist tradition, so that they can become full *bhikkhunīs* (Buddhist nun).

Born Chatsumarn Shatsena in Thailand in 1944, Bhikkhunī Dhammananda was a renowned scholar of Buddhism for more than 30 years, as well as a successful TV host. When she sought to be ordained as a full nun, she had to travel to Taiwan first and then to Sri Lanka because Thailand does not allow women's higher ordination. She was finally able to be ordained as a Theravāda *bhikkhunī* in 2003.

She is now the abbot of Songdhammakalyani temple near Bangkok, where she continues to write about the issue of ordination for women in the Theravāda and Tibetan traditions, and welcomes women seeking ordination.

Despite facing strong opposition from the Thai monastic institution, Dhammananda has continued to demonstrate patience and perseverance in pursuing her goal, and her work has become increasingly recognized and supported both locally and internationally.

305   Be patient. It's good for you!

Patience plays an important role in self-regulation, the ability to manage our behaviours and emotions, as well as direct our attention. People with high self-regulation are disciplined and intentional in their daily behaviours. Crucially, they are patient: they are able to give up immediate gratification for longer-term results. Unlike Willy Wonka in the Chocolate Factory, they don't want it *now*, they want it when – and if – it is appropriate.

Research shows that people with high self-regulation are better able to control their emotions and achieve their goals. They have fewer symptoms of anxiety and depression, and they also tend to be more professionally and socially successful.

So… hurry… be patient… it's good for you!

306   I haven't given up smoking. I've been putting it off for 25 years

Is there a habit you've been trying to get rid of for a long time? Try patience. Next time the urge to engage in that habit occurs, wait five minutes before giving in. If you can do five minutes, why don't you try another five? See how patient you can be before you give in.

The trick is to just wait. You're not *not* engaging in the habit, or giving it up, you're just telling your habit to wait for five minutes. Who knows? It might get tired of waiting and just go away.

307   Drop by drop

Just as the water pot is filled drop by drop, a wise one, practising little by little, is filled with merit.

The Buddha, *The Dhammapada*, 122

308   Are you patient enough?

How patient are you? Do you wish you had more patience? Less? Are there occasions when you are more patient than others? What characteristics do these occasions have in common? How does being patient or impatient affect you and those around you? Be precise and detailed in your descriptions.

What have you learned from this exercise? What intentions can you put into practice from it?

309   Be uncomfortable

I am a big fan of historical fiction. I love reading about people's daily lives in the past, about what they ate, how they slept and how they related to the world around them.

I find it especially remarkable how people in the past seemed to have a surprising ability to tolerate pain and discomfort. Granted, they did not have a choice. They lacked the medical knowledge and technology available today, but they seemed more patient with discomfort than we are in the modern world.

We reject the slightest bit of physical or mental pain. Yet, being able to bear moderate levels of discomfort helps us cultivate self-control and discipline. Some Buddhist monks and nuns, for example, only eat solid food before noon and fast the rest of the day, tolerating hunger pangs and cravings as part of their monastic training.

Although most of us don't need to give up eating for half the day, being more patient with slight discomfort can be a rewarding mindfulness practice in your daily life.

310   Testing the lady's patience

It is easy to have patience when everything is going well. The Buddha tells a story of a lady who was reputed for being patient and calm. Her maid wanted to find out whether the lady's reputation was well earned or whether her patience had never been tested – according to the maid herself, she fulfilled her chores so perfectly that the lady had nothing to be displeased with.

To test the lady, the maid got up very late one morning. The lady scolded her mildly. The next day, the maid got up even later and the lady scolded her more harshly. This continued for a few days until the lady was so infuriated that she hit the maid on the head and slightly cut her. The maid finally had her answer!

The Buddha tells this story to show how true patience exists only in the face of adversity. To develop patience, he says, you must consider agreeable and disagreeable events in a spirit of equanimity, realizing that all things eventually pass and therefore need not be a source of frustration or anger.

311   A matter of attitude

As the common saying goes, patience is not about your ability to wait but about your attitude while you wait. Actually, the Buddhist virtue of patience even includes qualities of endurance and forbearance in its description of patience. Patience is the virtue we demonstrate when we endure the bad temper of our teenager without giving in to bad temper ourselves. Or when we accept the punctured tyre without frustration.

Furthermore, patience is the ability to put difficulties in perspective, to ask yourself the question: 'Does this really warrant frustration or anger?'

In other words, patience is the attitude that recognizes that stuff happens and throwing a tantrum won't make it better.

312 Wait!

Develop the habit of waiting.

Are you hungry and want to eat? Wait 10 or 15 minutes before you act on your hunger. Do you want to buy an item of clothing or a new gadget? Wait three or four days, or even a week, before you get it. Are you feeling angry and want to yell at your partner or your co-worker? Bite your tongue, take a few deep breaths and remove yourself from the situation.

Waiting is good for you. It flexes the patience muscle (I'm sure you didn't know there was such a thing!). It delays gratification and helps you develop self-discipline. And it doesn't require you to do anything but wait.

313 A two-handed saw

The Buddha once described the virtue of patience by telling his assembly of monks that, even if bandits should carve them up limb by limb with a two-handed saw, or hit them with sticks and stones, or cut them up with knives, they should not feel anger. They should, on the contrary, calm their mind and body and develop mindfulness. They should speak no harsh words but instead arouse sympathy and goodwill towards the bandits.

Even though the analogy is rather strained to my twenty-first-century ears, it serves to illuminate how we relate to perceived offences. If you replace bandits with internet trolls and two-handed saws, sticks, stones and knives with negative comments and all the other offences you are regularly confronted with, you can heed the Buddha's advice to calm your mind and body and develop mindfulness and goodwill.

314 Feel the ground under your feet

Make a resolution. This week, whenever you start feeling impatient, even in the slightest, pause. Be present to the moment. Feel the ground under your feet, the seat under your bottom, the cloth against your skin. Feel your body from the inside. If anything is tight or tense, release it.

Now, focus on the impatience. What does it feel like in your body? Where is it located? What sensations are you experiencing? Is it heavy or light? Warm or cold? Tight or wobbly? Is it expanding or contracting?

Breathe deeply. Feel the air in your lungs as you inhale and exhale. Breathe into the feeling of impatience until it dissipates.

315   A plan to be patient

Patience is associated with the ability to self-regulate our behaviours and to be disciplined. What area of your life do you wish to be more patient in? What would it mean to be more patient in that area of your life? What results will it have on you and those around you when you succeed in being more patient? Can you outline precise and detailed steps to cultivate patience in that specific context?

316   No need for that! The extraordinary life of Ōtagaki Rengetsu

Ōtagaki Rengetsu (Lotus Moon) practised martial arts, wrote poetry and painted art but earned her living mostly by making pottery. Born in 1791 in Japan, she was adopted by a high-ranking aristocratic family that gave her a samurai education. Her first marriage was unhappy, but her husband died early and she finally found a beloved companion in her second husband. However, misfortune struck and she lost her adoptive parents and siblings, and several of her children, before her husband also died.

Following these tragedies, she became a Buddhist nun. That was when she started supporting herself by making pottery, which she called 'poorly crafted rough little things'. However, her idea of inscribing them with her poems made them so unusual that they became highly prized and became a style, named Rengetsu after her, that is still recognized today.

Her poetry is suffused with delicate and tender allusions to her losses and sadness and yet still shines with her forbearance and resilience. In one poem, she notices that she had become absorbed in thoughts of her lost children and, sternly reminding herself to enjoy the present moment, exclaims, 'No need for that!'

317   What's the rush?

Have you noticed how time has shrunk? Depending on when you were born, you might have had to wait for the weekend to go shopping. Mail came in only once a day and not every minute. Phones were stuck at home on the wall and did not intrude into every moment of our lives. You might have had to open a dictionary to check a word or go to the library to check the encyclopedia. Depending on where you grew up, eating out was a luxury that occurred only a few times a year, and food delivery was unknown.

But ask yourself: What's the rush? Do you need every single thing that pops into your mind to be delivered within 24 hours? Do you need to have your every whim fulfilled instantly?

Develop a practice of patience. Every time you want to order something or want to check a piece of information online, ask yourself if it can wait. And then, wait.

318   Don't react. Respond

Psychologists have highlighted the difference between reacting and responding. Reacting is immediate, unthinking, often based on preconceived ideas and without regard to consequences. Responding is slower, more thoughtful, in line with deeply held values and based on a careful appraisal of the situation and its possible consequences.

When we cultivate patience, we aim to respond to situations rather than react.

We pause.

We assess.

We reflect.

We respond.

Mindfulness strengthens our ability to become aware of the gap between an event and our reaction to it. The more proficient we become at noticing this gap, the more patient we become and the more able we are to respond rather than react.

319   What is the point of worrying?

If something can be done about it, what is the point of worrying?
If nothing can be done about it, what is the point of worrying?

Śāntideva (685–763 CE), *The Bodhicaryāvatāra*

320   Let go of too much

Many of us are often managing or, more likely, trying to manage several things at once – ferrying the kids to one of their many activities or checking in on elderly parents while replying to work emails and getting dinner ready. It's no surprise that the smallest thing can sweep us into a whirlpool of anger and frustration.

Take a moment or two and make a list of all the things you do day after day. Pat yourself on the back for achieving so much. Remind yourself that there are only 24 hours in a day and you really should spend eight of those sleeping.

Let go of what is too much.

321   Spectator of your own mind

Being mindful helps you develop your patience by allowing you to notice urges to act before thinking and to then act intentionally and purposefully.

In mindfulness meditation, you are encouraged to observe your perceptions, sensations, emotions, feelings and thoughts without reacting to them. You observe them and acknowledge them non-judgementally. They are not good or bad, they just are.

Further, you don't act on them. Is your left cheek itchy? Don't scratch it. Observe the sensation. Notice its extent, its quality and its intensity. Are you hungry? Observe the hunger. Where does it happen in your body? What does it feel like? Are you bored? Observe the feeling. Is it heavy or light? Diffuse or dense?

Little by little, being mindful helps you develop the patience to stay with whatever is happening as an attentive and kind spectator.

322   The Day of Miracles

A Tibetan Buddhist holiday, the Day of Miracles closes the two-week festival that starts with Losar, the Tibetan New Year. The Day of Miracles celebrates an episode in the life of the Buddha during which he defeated and converted followers of other teachers (often called the 'matted-hair ascetics' for their long, unkempt hair) who had been challenging him to show his supernatural powers.

The Buddha rarely displayed magical powers because he felt that it would attract people to his teachings for the wrong reasons. At some point, though, he realized that they would not give up asking him to do magic and this was causing turmoil and unease in the monastic community. The Buddha therefore performed extraordinary miracles that surpassed anything the matted-hair ascetics had ever done.

Tibetan Buddhists usually celebrate this day by attending religious events and observing precepts more strictly. Some teachers, such as the American nun Thubten Chödron, advise to reflect on the story of the Buddha's miracles as a source of inspiration on ways to respond to frustrations and provocations in a thoughtful and measured manner.

What are your supernatural powers?

323   How to be patient with yourself

Being patient with others is a good quality to have. However, we rarely think of being patient with ourselves. We often want to achieve results instantly and get frustrated when our efforts do not bear immediate fruit.

Describe how you are impatient with yourself. How can you cultivate more patience towards yourself? How would being more patient affect your experience?

324   What sets you off?

If you want to cultivate patience, you need to know what makes you impatient.

Develop the habit of noting when something makes you feel impatient. What are the circumstances? Who is involved? How does the feeling of impatience manifest in your body?

Identify what these moments have in common and plan to respond with more patience – kind attention and spaciousness. For example, if you get impatient when your child yet again is running late in the morning, think about ways to help them prepare the night before so that you can all leave on time. If you get impatient with a chatty co-worker (or your significant other if you're working from home), think about a response that acknowledges their need for connection and your desire to get back to work.

Where else do you need a little more patience?

325 The present moment

Do not yearn after the past or fantasize about the future.
The past is left behind. The future is yet to come.
See the present moment right here
Notice as the moment arises
Not beguiled or flustered
This is how to cultivate wisdom.
Today you should endeavour
Tomorrow, who knows? Death may come.

The Buddha, *The Bhadekaratta Sutta, Majjhima Nikāya*, 131

326 *Now*

Impatience manifests as the desire for things to be other than they are. We want something we don't have *now*. We want things to change *now*. We want our discomfort to stop *now*. Yet, things are the way they are *now*.

Mindfulness is the practice of seeing what is there *now* and accepting it as it is *now*. This does not mean that we don't try to change it. There is no reason we should accept pain, injustice or poverty. But accepting that it exists *now* allows us to move towards change.

The first Buddhist truth is recognizing that there is suffering *now*. Once you accept this truth, you can begin changing.

327 Comfort culture

Many of us live in a comfort culture. Many of us do very little physical work. We walk or run almost only as a leisure activity. In many places, we have heating in the winter and air conditioning in the summer. We have painkillers for the slightest ache. We replace hips and knees as though they were shirts.

Although many of these things are good and have improved life conditions for many people in wealthy countries, and for the wealthy all over the world, they come at a price. They leave us unprepared for facing what the Buddha called the first Noble Truth, the fact that being alive inevitably entails suffering at some point or another.

Acknowledging this reality in the smaller things can help us prepare better for the bigger and ineluctable ones – the accidents and illnesses that we, or our loved ones, will certainly encounter, the slow unravelling that comes with ageing and, finally, the loss of loved ones. These too are part of life.

328 The most heroic of virtues

Patience is the most heroic of virtues, precisely because
it does not appear to be heroic at all.

Giacomo Leopardi (1798–1837), *Zibaldone di pensieri*

329 Touch

Do you have a moment? Sit down. Set a timer and stay still. For as long as you can afford to, but determine not to stop before the timer goes off.

Close your eyes. Take a few deep breaths. Focus on the sensations on your skin.

Start with your face. What can you feel? Your eyelids protecting your eyes? Relax them. The air on your cheeks? Smooth them out. Your tongue inside your mouth? Unhinge your jaw.

Continue examining your body and the sensations that tell you where you are in space. The points of pressure. The clothes on your skin. The vibrating, quivering, throbbing, pulsating, radiating, twisting, gurgling inside your body. Stay focused on the sensations in your body and bring your attention back to them when it wanders.

What else can you touch?

330   Put up with it

One of the aspects of patience is forbearance. Forbearance is the ability to tolerate what we don't want or don't enjoy or, even better, to put up with it with grace and kindness.

Why would we want to put up with the things we don't want or don't enjoy? I am not recommending that you put up with pain, harm, abuse or injustice, but simply with the small inconveniences of daily life.

Is your nephew throwing a tantrum because your sister is not giving in to his demands? Take a few breaths and keep that comment on her parenting skills to yourself. Is the waiter a bit rude and unfriendly? Ask him how his day is going – he may be having a tough time, and kindness might be exactly what he needs (plus a good tip!).

You're putting up with these things because you realize that life is tough not just for you but for those around you too, and your goal is to offer them, and yourself, some respite.

CHAPTER 12
COMPASSION

331   Compassion

In Buddhist sources, compassion is described as the 'grounding of buddhahood' or, in other words, one of the fundamental virtues of a buddha. It is said that the Buddha undertook his spiritual path and his teaching out of compassion for all beings.

At its most basic, compassion is the ability to understand and empathize with others' suffering and to act on the desire to remove or alleviate it. Note that it's not merely empathy but an active desire to help end the suffering of others.

In fact, Buddhist texts compare it to the feelings of a mother when her child is sick. She does not just empathize with the child but actively endeavours to relieve their suffering.

How have you cultivated this feeling in the past? How can you cultivate it now?

332   Try their shoes on

To develop compassion for others, we must see their perspective and understand how they see the world. Philosopher Bertrand Russell, writing about examining other philosophers' ideas, argued that it is necessary to read their work with sympathy until we understand what it is like to believe in their theories.

Likewise, practise understanding what another person believes, feels or experiences: listen with sympathy until you are able to appreciate what it is like for them. As the saying goes, before judging someone, walk a mile in their shoes.

333   Save all beings

Avalokiteśvara is the bodhisattva of compassion. In Mahāyāna Buddhism, the form of Buddhism practised in East Asia (China, Korea,

Japan, Tibet, Mongolia and Vietnam), bodhisattvas are beings who vow to become buddhas and work for the welfare of all beings.

Avalokiteśvara is said to help every being who needs it, often saving them from drowning or from fire. In Tibet, Avalokiteśvara is called Chenrezig, and is often represented with a thousand arms to symbolize his unceasing activity in helping others. In the East, Avalokiteśvara is often portrayed in female form, and his name is translated as Kuan Yin (or Guanyin) in China and Kannon in Japan.

Avalokiteśvara is the bodhisattva who hears the cries of those who suffer and takes any form necessary to provide succour and assistance. In his many forms across the world, Avalokiteśvara offers a refuge when in need.

What do Avalokiteśvara's story and character evoke for you?

334   What is compassion for you?

What is compassion for you? When and how have you encountered it?

Remember an instance when you have acted on your compassion for someone, or have been the recipient of someone's compassion. Describe in detail what the situation was and what happened. Be specific and thorough. How did it make you feel? What emotions, feelings and thoughts were present?

What emotions, feelings and thoughts arise in the present moment from remembering this episode?

335   *Bodhicitta*

In Buddhism, compassion is the primary motivation of a Buddha and, by extension, of all Buddhists. The desire to remove or alleviate the suffering of all beings – of oneself and others – is what gets us on the Buddhist path.

In Mahāyāna Buddhism, this is called *bodhicitta*, the 'mind of awakening'. When someone develops *bodhicitta*, they feel and act out of a very deep wish to treat others with kindness and to endeavour for the welfare of all beings.

At an ordinary level, every time you act with kindness towards yourself, or towards others, you water the *bodhicitta* seed in you. Eventually, the seed will grow into the tree of compassion. How much water will you give your tree of compassion?

336   Let it be enough

All those who are unhappy are unhappy for seeking
their own happiness.

All those who are happy are happy for seeking the
happiness of others.

What is the point of saying more?

Let it be enough to compare the fool who seeks only their
own benefit and the wise who seeks only that of others.

Śāntideva (685–763 CE), *Bodhicaryāvatāra*

337   Real people

Research shows that we feel compassion more easily for real people than for an abstract group. Stanford University psychologist Brian Knutson and his colleagues led an experiment in which people were shown pictures of children. Some were shown photographs of real children; others were shown silhouettes or names. They were then encouraged to donate part of the payment they had received for participating in the study to an organization for children's welfare. Participants who had been shown photographs of real children were much more likely to donate than those who had been shown only silhouettes or names.

To cultivate compassion for a group of people, think about the reality behind the group – the very real individuals that make up the group. The next time you talk to the bank teller, or when you see other commuters on your way to work, look at them as individuals with families and histories. Imagine them going about their daily lives to make them more real and less abstract, and to develop a strong sense of their humanity.

338   Exchanging self for others

Tonglen is a Tibetan practice that aims to awaken and cultivate compassion in a very real way by 'exchanging self for others': we take in the suffering of others, and we send them relief and loving kindness.

In this meditation, it is customary to start with someone close to you and then to extend the practice to all beings who are suffering. Start by visualizing the person and breathe in their suffering (in the form of a cloud, for example) and send out love and relief (in the form of light and warmth, for example).

Meditation teacher Pema Chödron suggests starting with yourself and your own suffering (so that your own suffering is also taken into account) and then gradually extending the practice to those who suffer in similar ways.

339   Do not hate: the Dalai Lama and the Chinese

Tenzin Gyatso, the 14th Dalai Lama, is a well-known figure of contemporary Buddhism. The 1989 Nobel Peace Prize recipient was born in 1935 as Lhamo Thondup, the son of a farmer in north-eastern Tibet. At the age of two, he was recognized as the incarnation of the previous Dalai Lama, a unique Tibetan institution in which highly spiritually realized people are said to choose where and when to be reborn. The Dalai Lamas are believed to be emanations of Avalokiteśvara, the bodhisattva of compassion.

The 14th Dalai Lama has indeed been a living embodiment of compassion for many decades despite the difficulties he, and fellow Tibetans, have had to confront. Forced by the Chinese invasion to flee Tibet in 1959, he found refuge in Dharamsala, in India, where he has lived since. From there, and in his travels around the world, the Dalai Lama has been a voice for peace, calling the Chinese his brothers and sisters and pleading for a peaceful resolution that recognizes and protects the people of Tibet and its unique culture and religion.

For him, 'You must not hate those who do wrong or harmful things; but with compassion, you must do what you can to stop them – for they are harming themselves, as well as those who suffer from their actions.'

340   A meditation practice

Many Buddhists practise a form of meditation that extends compassion to all beings. First, you start with yourself, thinking, 'May I feel well, may I be safe, may I be healthy and free from suffering, may I be happy.' Then you think of someone you love very dearly, thinking, 'May you feel well, may you be safe, may you be healthy and free from suffering, may you be happy.' Depending on how much time you have, you can increase the number of people or stay focused on one or two.

As you repeat the words silently to yourself, bring to mind a vivid image of the person you are focusing on, as if they were sitting in front of you, and then picture what wellbeing, safety, health and happiness may be for them. Finally, visualize them feeling well, safe, healthy and happy.

I like to imagine that I wish myself and others to be psychologically well, to be safe from external dangers, to be physically and mentally healthy, and finally to be content.

Traditionally, it's customary to end the meditation by extending good wishes to all beings. Why don't you try it?

341   Active compassion

What differentiates compassion from empathy is its active component. While empathy is being aware of the suffering of others, compassion is not only being aware but also actively seeking to remove or alleviate their suffering. This, of course, applies to self-compassion as well.

Describe a difficult situation in which you, or someone you know, find yourselves and describe in which ways that situation could be improved. Be as specific as you can and as imaginative as possible, from a small, helpful thing (for example, a hug) to the most outlandish (be creative here). You are exploring ideas in this space, so you don't have to be limited in what is possible. Sometimes, inspired solutions come from not letting oneself be constrained by perceived limitations.

Once you are done with this exercise, choose one action that you can do to help with the situation *right now*.

342   Sentient beings like me

I should dispel the suffering of others because their suffering
is like my own suffering.

I should help others too because they are sentient beings like me.
Śāntideva (685–763 CE), *Bodhicaryāvatāra*

343   Life is too short

Life is simply too short to be mean, either to yourself or to others. Something happens? Be mindful: There is annoyance. There is irritation. There is suffering. Remember: stuff happens – that's the nature of existence, according to Buddhism.

Be present to your annoyance, to your irritation, to your suffering. How does it feel in the body? Where is it located? Recognize that it's difficult.

Cheer yourself up a bit. If it helps, hold yourself as you would a child, or a dear friend. Remember: it will pass.

344   Self-compassion

Self-compassion is simply directing compassion towards oneself. With self-compassion, we turn the feeling of empathy we have for those who are suffering towards ourselves.

Psychologist and researcher Kristin Neff tells us to cultivate self-compassion by focusing on three main aspects. First, recognize our common humanity. You are not alone in your suffering – all human beings suffer at one point or another. When dealing with self-criticism, it's helpful to remember that we are all imperfect and to give yourself a break.

Secondly, treat yourself with kindness, just as you would a very dear friend – talk to yourself as you would this dear friend who is in physical or mental pain.

Finally, to do all this, develop mindfulness, a caring, accepting and non-judgemental attitude towards yourself that allows you to be present to your need for self-compassion.

345   Be self-compassionate, radically

This is a challenge to practise radical self-compassion. Give yourself a day, today for example, and commit to be fully compassionate to yourself.

Every time your critical inner voices speak to you, thank them for being there and remind them that nobody is perfect, that messiness is the stuff of life, and that to be fully human is to be beautifully and uniquely imperfect.

Then, treat yourself as you would a dear friend. Give yourself the attention and kindness you would a friend who's being overly self-critical.

Try it out and see how it feels.

346   Be mindful, be compassionate

In Buddhism, wisdom and mindfulness are intrinsically related to compassion. One cannot be developed without the other. As wisdom is developed, compassion arises. And compassion needs wisdom to blossom.

This means that we need wisdom to feel compassion because it helps us see the suffering in ourselves and others. We also need compassion to be mindful; otherwise we risk becoming detached or judgemental.

Compassion helps us be mindful of all things in ourselves and in others with an accepting and caring attitude. Wisdom allows us to understand the source of suffering and to provide support when possible.

How do you see this playing out in your life?

347   Be kind to yourself

Cultivating self-compassion is not easy but it is well worth it. Research in psychology indicates that a lack of self-compassion can lead to anxiety and depression, and that greater self-compassion is associated with higher resilience, self-motivation, health-supporting behaviours and pro-social attitudes.

Psychologists suggest developing a self-compassion practice, either as a formal meditation or as a moment in the day when you remember to treat yourself with kindness and understanding, so that when a difficult moment arises, you are already accustomed to being compassionate to yourself and more able to give yourself care and kindness.

348 Love is the deepest revolution: bell hooks

Thinker and author bell hooks is well known as a feminist and anti-racist activist, as well as for her work to build the 'beloved community' dreamed of by Dr Martin Luther King, Jr. Born in the rural Southern United States in 1952, Gloria Jean Watkins chose the name bell hooks in honour of her grandmother, written without capital letters to emphasize her ideas rather than herself. She started writing her book *Ain't I a Woman: Black women and feminism* at 19, when she was still in college, and published more than 30 books on a range of themes, from US history, Black feminism and Black masculinity to teaching, love and friendship.

As a university professor, she saw teaching as an act of love and connection, and she intentionally avoided the formal academic style of her colleagues at Yale, Oberlin or the University of Southern California. Spirituality was deeply important to her. She described herself as a Buddhist Christian, and often met with Zen teacher Thich Nhat Hanh. Based on his advice to move beyond anger, she came to believe that anger should be used as the compost that energizes the work to seek justice.

For bell hooks, love was the 'deepest revolution… one healing heart, giving and sustaining life… our hope and our salvation'.

349 Write yourself a letter

Imagine that a dear friend has encountered a difficulty in their life. Maybe they failed an exam, or their relationship ended, or they didn't get the job they wanted, or they lost someone dear to them.

Imagine you are writing them a letter. What would you write to them? How would you try to comfort them and be supportive of them?

Keep the letter. When you encounter a difficulty, read it to yourself.

350   Other beings to work for

The 14th Dalai Lama once said that our spiritual development depends upon others because we can only nurture qualities such as compassion, love, tolerance and generosity in relation to others. He used the example of the Buddha, who was encouraged to start teaching because other beings needed his transformative understanding.

In fact, Buddhist sources say that the Buddha was inclined to rest in his profound realization when the god Brahma visited him to petition him. Brahma told the Buddha that there were many beings ready and willing to hear his teachings and that, for their benefit, he must teach.

When have you felt that your contribution was required for others' wellbeing or progress?

351   You don't know what that person is going through

The great eleventh-century Indian Buddhist philosopher Atiśa argued that since we have lived innumerable lives and have been born in countless forms of life, at one point or another every living being must have been our mother and given us their love and kindness. This is why, Atiśa said, we should treat every living being as though they were our mother and repay their kindness with our care and affection.

In the contemporary world, Buddhist teachers recommend treating others as though they were dear friends. Or, at the very least, as a sign hung at my local café says, 'Be kind, you don't know what that person is going through.'

352   Put your oxygen mask on first

For some people compassion might be *too* appealing: people who are always generous, who always put others ahead of themselves and forget their own needs and wellbeing, may end up depleted and exhausted.

If you are such a person, shine some mindfulness on these moments when you want to say yes to another request for help, when you want to be helpful and supportive at too great a cost to yourself.

Remember: put your own oxygen mask on first.

353 Don't be perfect; be human

Despite a French saying warning that 'perfection is the enemy of the good', perfectionism is seen in many cultures as a virtue. Yet, I am sure you can think of the many ways in which perfectionism has stood in the way of good outcomes.

A study by British researchers Tom Curran and Andrew Hill showed that the steady increase of perfectionism since 1989 among British, Canadian and American students has had a range of detrimental effects. For one, perfectionists feel a lot of stress and shame and they can develop avoidant coping strategies that eventually result in what they fear most: failure. Perfectionism prevents us from even trying because of a fear of not being perfect. For another, perfectionists are rarely satisfied with what they accomplish and this can lead to harsh self-criticism and eventually depression.

One way to address perfectionism is to recognize our basic humanity. Being human *is* being imperfect. Remind yourself of this simple fact: we *all* slip up, blunder, bomb, flunk, misstep, fail to live up to our standards or, in other words, f*** up.

354 You're not alone

If you find it difficult to treat yourself with compassion, you are not alone. Many people find self-compassion difficult and even unnatural.

Try seeing yourself as a small child, or even as a baby, if that makes it easier to be gentle and loving to yourself. Remember that life is often tough and painful, and you're not alone to suffer. Treat yourself like a dear friend and be supportive rather than critical.

Cultivate this self-compassion practice to use in difficult moments and to achieve a greater sense of self-acceptance and wellbeing.

355   Asanga's compassion

The Indian Buddhist philosopher Asanga is known for his great compassion as well as for being the founder of the Yogācāra ('mind-only') school of Buddhism that claims that all that exists is the endless flow of consciousness.

According to the tradition, Asanga was born in the fourth century, in the kingdom of Gandhāra (now in Pakistan). After becoming a monk, and a long period studying, he went on retreat in the hope of having a vision of Maitreya, the Buddha of the future. He spent many years meditating in a cave, but not encountering success, he decided to give up.

As he was leaving his cave, he met an old mangy dog whose wounded leg was infested with maggots. Legend says that Asanga was filled with great compassion for the dog and, more extraordinarily, for the maggots. He resolved to cut off a piece of his own thigh to place the maggots on and to remove them with his tongue instead of his fingers, so that he wouldn't harm them.

As he was about to carry out his plan, the dog disappeared and Maitreya appeared. He explained to Asanga that he had been there all along, but that Asanga could not see him until his great compassion finally cleared his understanding. Maitreya then took Asanga to the heavens and taught him the Yogācāra, which Asanga brought back to the human realm.

Asanga's act of great compassion reminds us that, when we see beyond the separation between you and me, between your suffering and mine, we can touch the divine.

356   Be your own best friend

Bring to mind a difficult episode or event in your life. Remember what it was like. Be specific in your description. Where was it? When? Who did it involve? What did you do? What did you think? What feelings and emotions were present? How did you treat yourself?

Imagine you could be there and talk to yourself. What would you say to comfort and support your past self?

Self-compassion includes being kind to ourselves and mindful of what is happening within us, and remembering that we're not alone. Be your own best friend. Be there for yourself.

357   The circle of compassion

Physicist and Nobel Prize winner Albert Einstein (1879–1955) once said that we must widen our circle of compassion to include all living creatures and nature. As human beings we are only a limited part of the universe, he explained, and while we experience ourselves as separate from the rest of the universe, it is only an 'optical illusion of [our] consciousness'. The result is that we confine ourselves to our own desires and only care for those close to us.

How will you expand your circle of compassion?

358   Have tea with your fears

Zen teacher Thich Nhat Hanh had his own take on a canonical Buddhist story in which the Buddha is regularly visited by Māra, the Buddhist personification of all evils. Māra is basically always trying to get rid of the Buddha and his teachings by trying to convince him to depart this life.

Thich Nhat Hanh imagines the Buddha welcoming Māra, inviting him for tea and having a little chat with him. 'Māra, how is it going? It must be pretty tough to be Māra all the time! Thanks for visiting.'

Likewise, when you are visited by fears, anxieties and other negative thoughts, invite them in, offer them some tea or coffee, be there with them for a moment, thank them for their visit and let them go.

359 Self-esteem or self-compassion?

In her book *Self-Compassion*, Kristin Neff differentiates between self-esteem and self-compassion. Self-esteem, she says, is an evaluation of our worthiness that is relative and contingent. This makes it unreliable as a source of wellbeing since it is bound to change depending on the situation or context.

Self-compassion, meanwhile, is founded on recognizing our intrinsic worthiness as human beings. As such, we have both strengths and weaknesses, but that does not detract from our worthiness.

Practise accepting that you are not perfect, it will help you develop self-compassion.

360 Master Juzhi Yizhi raises a finger

Whenever the great Chinese Chan (Zen) master Juzhi Yizhi (Gutei in Japanese), who lived in the ninth century, was asked a question about Buddhism, he simply raised a finger in answer, baffling the enquirer.

Was he telling them to be quiet? Was he pointing to the 'suchness' of all things, the idea that all things ultimately partake of the same nature or, as Sengcan (Sôsan), another great Chinese master, said, 'one is all,

all is one'? Was he suggesting that the requester could find the answer in their own heart if only they listened to it?

One story says that a young boy at Juzhi's monastery took to following the master's example and that, every time someone spoke to him, he would also raise his finger. Juzhi heard of the boy and asked him if it were so. The boy stuck up his finger. Juzhi grabbed him and, in his great compassion, cut off all his fingers. The boy, it is said, attained awakening in that moment.

What do you make of Juzhi's teaching methods?

CHAPTER 13

FIVE CORE IDEAS

361   Accept life

The Buddha summarized his teachings with the succinct statement that he taught suffering and the end of suffering. Suffering is unavoidable. When we resist what is happening, we create additional suffering that is avoidable – what is sometimes called 'the suffering of suffering'.

When we live mindfully, we focus on the present moment and we embrace it fully. When we embrace what is there fully, we avoid the suffering of suffering. To avoid the suffering of suffering, says Zen master Thich Nhat Hanh, we need to realize that the conditions for our happiness are already here right now.

What are the conditions of your happiness?

In a nutshell, if you are reading this, you are alive and, in this moment, all possibilities are present. All the possibilities to live your life as you want it are already present.

Recognize that your life is what it is now. Accept it. From this moment on, live the life you want to live. It may not always be easy, and you will not always succeed, but it's only by *accepting* life as it is now that you can *live* it fully.

362   Be kind

Be kind to yourself. Be kind to others.

Be kind to yourself. That doesn't mean being self-indulgent. It means taking good care of yourself and those around you and, more widely, of the world.

Be kind to others. There is no doubt that what's most important in life are our connections to others. It's also the most difficult challenge we will face. Since we cannot have a good connection to others if we don't have a good connection to ourselves, we must start with ourselves.

So be kind to yourself. Treat yourself well. Sleep enough. Exercise. Eat your vegetables. Find a moment or two to practise a mindful activity, whether it's meditation, chanting mantras or yoga (the meditative sort of yoga).

Treat others well. Assume the best. Give the benefit of the doubt. Be generous. Keep your promises. Be the good friend you want to have to yourself and to others.

In short, show compassion and loving kindness to yourself and to others.

363   Be present

Use all your senses to be present in the here and now. Bring your mind and body together as often as you can.

What can you see, hear, touch, taste, smell right here, right now? What's in your mind right now? What thoughts and emotions are there?

Just acknowledge them one by one, without letting yourself be carried away by the story they tell.

When you attend to your senses, you ground yourself in the present moment. You weave the fabric of your life moment by moment. Hold on to the thread.

364   Pay attention to your attention

What is on your mind right now? These words? What you need to do today or tomorrow? An argument you had with your partner or your child? An upcoming meeting?

Spend a moment examining your mind and what's in it. That's it! You're paying attention to your attention.

British scholar of Buddhist philosophy Paul Williams calls this the reflective nature of awareness. Think of it as a mirror. When you pay attention to your attention, you become aware of the content of your mind. This kind of awareness is neutral. It doesn't reject, grasp or judge. It just reflects what is there, just like a mirror reflects what is in front of it.

Once you are aware of the content of your mind and know where your attention is, it becomes easier to place your attention where you want it to be.

365   Let go of judgement

Being mindful means being aware of what goes on in our mind and body, in our life, in our environment, moment by moment and, most crucially, without judgement. And without judgement of judgement.

Our brain is wired to judge and predict everything. We are constantly evaluating what is happening inside and outside of us. Mindfulness is about dropping the inner judge. Don't judge the judge either! It's doing its job of keeping you safe. Thank it when it makes a comment, but no more than that.

Try it out. See how it feels to stop the judging. And to stop the judging of the judging.

Things are what they are. *That* is *nirvāṇa*, the end of suffering.

REFERENCES AND FURTHER READING

To learn more about Buddhism

Caplow, F. and Moon, S. (Eds.). (2013). *The Hidden Lamp: Stories from Twenty-Five Centuries of Awakened Women*. Wisdom Publications.

Engelmajer, P. (2013). *Buddhism*. Hodder & Stoughton.

Hanh, T. N. (2014). *No Mud, No Lotus: The Art of Transforming Suffering*. Parallax Press.

hooks, b. (2021). Toward a worldwide culture of love. *Lion's Roar*, June 8. Accessible at https://www.lionsroar.com/toward-a-worldwide-culture-of-love/

Kornfield, J. (1993). *A Path with Heart: A Guide through the Perils and Promises of Spiritual Life*. Bantam.

Shaw, S. (2021). *The Art of Listening: A Guide to the Early Teachings of Buddhism*. Shambhala Publications.

Tsomo, K. L. (2014). *Eminent Buddhist Women*. SUNY.

Williams, P. (1989). *Mahāyāna Buddhism: The Doctrinal Foundations*. Routledge.

To learn more about secular mindfulness

Brewer, J. (2021). *Unwinding Anxiety: New Science Shows How to Break the Cycles of Worry and Fear to Heal Your Mind*. Avery.

Burkeman, O. (2013). *The Antidote: Happiness for People Who Can't Stand Positive Thinking*. Farrar, Straus and Giroux.

Burkeman, O. (2021). *Four Thousand Weeks: Time Management for Mortals*. Macmillan.

Jha, A. (2021). *Peak Mind: Find Your Focus, Own Your Attention, Invest 12 Minutes a Day*. HarperOne.

Neff, K. (2015). *Self-Compassion: The Proven Power of Being Kind to Yourself*. William Morrow. See also https://self-compassion.org/

Santos, L., *The Happiness Lab*. Pushkin Industries. https://www.happinesslab.fm/

Contemporary Buddhist and meditation teachers cited

Brach, Tara. https://www.tarabrach.com/

Chödron, Pema. https://pemachodronfoundation.org/

Khandro Rinpoche. http://mjkr.org/biography.cfm

International Network of Engaged Buddhists (INEB) https://www.inebnetwork.org/

McDonald, M. RAIN: *The Nourishing Art of Mindful Inquiry*. Tricycle Online Courses. https://learn.tricycle.org/p/rain

Siravaksa, S. (Ed.). (1994). *The Quest for a Just Society: The Work and Legacy of Buddhadasa Bhikkhu*. Thai Inter-Religious Commission for Development.

williams, angel Kyodo. https://angelkyodowilliams.com/bio/

Yongey Mingyur Rinpoche. https://tergar.org/

Other articles and books cited

Clear, J. (2018). *Atomic Habits: An Easy & Proven Way to Build Good Habits & Break Bad Ones*. Avery.

Curran, T. & Hill, A. (2019). Perfectionism is increasing over time: A meta-analysis of birth cohort differences from 1989 to 2016. *Psychological Bulletin*, 145(4), 410.

Darlington, S. M. (2012). *The Ordination of a Tree: The Thai Buddhist Environmental Movement*. SUNY Press.

Dores Cruz, T. D., Beersma, B., Dijkstra, M. T. M. & Bechtoldt, M. N. (2019). The bright and dark side of gossip for cooperation in groups. *Frontiers in Psychology*, June. Accessible at https://www.frontiersin.org/articles/10.3389/fpsyg.2019.01374/full

Hadot, P., Carlier, J. & Davidson, A. I. (2011). *The Present Alone is Our Happiness: Conversations with Jeannie Carlier and Arnold I. Davidson*. Cultural Memory in the Present. Stanford University Press.

Heim, M. (2014). *The Forerunner of All Things: Buddhaghosa on Mind, Intention and Agency*. Oxford University Press.

hooks, b. (1981). *Ain't I a Woman: Black Women and Feminism*. Pluto Press.

Jacobs, A. J. (2018). *Thanks a Thousand: A Gratitude Journey*. Simon & Schuster/TED.

Joseph, S., OBE, Chairperson, The Niwano Peace Prize Committee, Honorary President's Address for the 38th Niwano Peace Prize Awarded to the Venerable Shih Chao-hwei of Taiwan. https://www.npf.or.jp/english/wp-content/uploads/sites/2/2021/06/038th_honorary_president_j.pdf last accessed 2 June 2022.

Klein E., The Ezra Klein Show. *The New York Times*. Accessible at https://www.nytimes.com/2022/02/25/opinion/ezra-klein-podcast-c-thi-nguyen.html

Knutson, B., Genevsky, A., Västfjäll, D. & Slovic, P. (2013). Cognitive neural underpinnings of the identifiable victim effect: Affect shifts preferences for giving. *Journal of Neuroscience*, 23 October, *33*(43), 17188–96.

Nagoski A. & Nagoski, E. (2020). *Burnout: The Secret to Unlocking the Stress Cycle*. Penguin Random House.

Norton, M. I., Rudd, M. & Aaker, J. (2014). Getting the most out of giving: Concretely framing a presocial goal maximizes happiness. *Journal of Experimental Social Psychology*, September, 54, 11–24. Also see https://www.businesswire.com/news/home/20140722005515/en/Concrete-Acts-of-Kindness-Boost-Happiness-Shows-Research-from-Stanford-Graduate-School-of-Business

Oettingen, G. (2017). *Rethinking Positive Thinking Inside the New Science of Motivation*. Penguin Random House. Also see https://woopmylife.org/en/home

Russell, H. (2021). *How to be Sad: Everything I've Learned about Getting Happier by being Sad*. HarperOne.

Sorensen, M. (2014). Ma-chig Lab-dron: Mother of Tibetan Buddhist Chod. In T. Lewis (Ed.), *Buddhists: Understanding Buddhism Through the Lives of Practitioners*. Wiley.

Weil, S. (1970). *First and Last Notebooks*, trans. R. Rees. Oxford University Press.

williams, a. K., Owens, R. & Syedullah, J. (2017). *Radical Dharma: Talking Race, Love, and Liberation*. Read How You Want.

Willis, J. (2020). *Dharma Matters: Women, Race, and Tantra*. Wisdom Publications.

ACKNOWLEDGEMENTS

As with all things we do, this book would not have been possible without the presence, support and love of many. Here is a welcome opportunity to recognize a few of them publicly.

First, I want to thank Iain Campbell at Hachette UK for approaching me with the idea for this book, and for providing gentle guidance throughout the process of writing what is not typical academic prose. Many thanks also to the editorial team at John Murray Press (especially Meaghan Lim and Vivienne Church).

Anjali Thavendran and Don Chen read an early section of this book. I am very fortunate to have them as my friends and I want to thank them for their time and feedback, and Anjali, especially, for her kind praise and enthusiastic support. Whether it is writing or parenting, she is always encouraging when I need it most.

I am grateful to Sara Knowles for reading another early section of the book and above all for our Wednesday afternoon sit-and-bitch sessions – they keep me sane. And to Sara, and her wife, Elizabeth McCord, for the sharing of food, conversations and friendship.

I am indebted to Misa Izuhara for her translation of a poem by Rengetsu, and deeply grateful for her friendship over time and distance. Although the poem did not make it into the final version of this book, seeing the literal translation from the Japanese intensified for me the open *kôan* quality of Rengetsu's poetry which is not easy to render in English or French translations.

I am fortunate that David DiValerio was one of our very first friends here. He was also among the first to discuss writing non-academic books with me, and he suggested sources for Tibetan life stories. I am similarly grateful to my friend and colleague Abigail Markwyn for her warm collegial support and for exploring ways of writing beyond academia on many walks and tea breaks.

My mother, Lyliane Engelmajer-Rivera, provided me with an ongoing source of quotations and sustains me with her love and daily check-ins. *Merci d'être là.*

My son, Ziggy, does not need thanks for the many opportunities he gives me, not always unwittingly, to test much of the advice in this book, and this book is better for them. Ziggy, you are an immeasurable source of delight, joy and pride.

There are not enough words to thank my spouse, Massimo Rondolino, for his patience and support. He has read many drafts of this book and has not only searched for but also translated Tibetan, Sanskrit, Latin and Italian quotations for me. He nourishes my body with an endless supply of homemade sourdough bread and pastries and my soul with an endless supply of love and inspiration.

Thank you to the International Network of Engaged Buddhists Secretariat for granting permission to reproduce a quote from Venerable Bhikkhu Buddhadasa cited in Ajahn Sulak Sivaraksa, *The Quest for a Just Society: The Work and Legacy of Buddhadasa Bhikkhu* (Thai Inter-Religious Commission for Development, 1994).

Finally, I am grateful to the many teachers, authors, researchers, journalists, thinkers and philosophers who have inspired the best parts of this book. Everything else, as the customary disclaimer goes, is my own.

Pascale F. Engelmajer, Brookfield, June 2022

IT'S TIME TO SEIZE THE DAY.
ALL 365 OF THEM.

365 – your day-by-day guide to living better and working smarter

365 Ways to be More Stoic 978-1-52939-044-5

365 Ways to Develop Mental Toughness 978-1-52939-764-2

365 Ways to Save the Planet 978-1-52939-741-3

365 Ways to Live Mindfully 978-1-52939-039-1

365 Ways to Have a Good Day 978-1-52938-224-2

JOHN
MURRAY
LEARNING

Would you like your people to read this book?

If you would like to discuss how you could bring these ideas to your team, we would love to hear from you. Our titles are available at competitive discounts when purchased in bulk across both physical and digital formats. We can offer bespoke editions featuring corporate logos, customized covers, or letters from company directors in the front matter can also be created in line with your special requirements.

We work closely with leading experts and organizations to bring forward-thinking ideas to a global audience. Our books are designed to help you be more successful in work and life.

For further information, or to request a catalogue, please contact:
business@johnmurrays.co.uk
sales-US@nicholasbrealey.com (North America only)

John Murray Learning is an imprint of
John Murray Press.